MW00681481

Published by:

Jennasis & Associates

Printed in the United States of America

Contributor: Marsha Leest

Editor: Jessica Shaffalo

ISBN: 978-1-7329322-0-3

BUILDING BLOCKS

CASE STUDIES OF
A SERIAL ENTREPRENEUR

GARY SHAMIS

IN APPRECIATION

To my parents (of blessed memory), Marvin and Bernice Shamis,
who bestowed on me an appreciation for the right values.

And to my wife, Mary Ann, who encouraged me to practice these values.

TABLE OF CONTENTS

FOREWORD

When I first met Gary Shamis 20 years ago at a business conference, our professional connection was immediate. We were both working for fast-growing accounting firms—he with Saltz, Shamis & Goldfarb (SS&G), which would ultimately become the largest CPA firm in the state of Ohio; I as a partner with FERS, a Chicago startup that grew to be the thirteenth largest accounting firm in the country before we eventually sold to H&R Block.

However despite our instant connection, I had no idea just how influential Gary would go on to be in my life, personally as well as professionally. He would become not just one of my closest mentors and at-times business partner, but one of my closest friends. He taught me many life lessons that were crucial to my success, ultimately helping me to realize my goals as a thought leader, consultant and advisor to the accounting profession.

Now, with the release of *Building Blocks*, Gary is bringing these lessons to a new generation of aspiring entrepreneurs. With each chapter, you'll notice how everything he touches—for himself, as well as others—is focused on innovation. That's been his key to success from the start; one he's passed on to me, and now, will pass on to you.

Back in 1998 when we met, as the Managing Director for SS&G, his team was one of the first firms in the nation to move away from old school accounting to focus on client services, such as compliance and advising. He would go on to found entities to further drive this innovative focus across the industry, including LEA Global, which is now the second-largest international professional association; The Advisory Board, a CPA firm think tank; the Winning is Everything Conference, the most recognized and attended proprietary management conference in the country; and, most recently, Winding River Consulting, which helps accounting and consulting firm managing partners be successful.

With that kind of resume, it's no wonder Gary has been named an Ernst & Young Entrepreneur of the Year and one of the most influential accounting professionals of his time, among other accolades. Yet he'd be the last person to tell you that. Gary is altogether focused on helping others to reach their fullest potential.

In my more than 30 years in business, I've learned that people tend to fall into two general categories: givers and takers. There are plenty of takers in business, but Gary is one of those rare few individuals who truly is a giver. He possesses a unique ability to connect with others not just on business issues, but on an intimate level. And that's really what sets *Building Blocks* apart from other business advice books.

Building Blocks is a deep dive into entrepreneurialism, but with a personal touch that guides and instructs without ego. Gary, like any successful entrepreneur, has taken many risks—some of which panned out, some of which failed. But if I've learned anything from working with him over the past two decades, as well as through this book, it's this: if you're going to play the game of business, you are going to fail.

Gary doesn't hide or sugarcoat his failures, but instead highlights them with humor and humility as critical lessons along his path. In these pages, he unabashedly gives you the very essence of who he is and what he's been through in the hopes readers won't shy away from their own challenges. He shows you that success comes not from dwelling on your failures, but from maintaining the confidence in yourself to keep taking the next big risk and making tough decisions. It comes from always focusing ahead of you instead of behind.

In that way, Gary teaches entrepreneurs to look at things differently; to gain clarity on what they want to achieve, and to be a street fighter with class to get there. He also emphasizes that the most successful entrepreneurs are the ones who find balance in caring for others' success as well as their own, and in giving back to their communities.

With all due respect to colleges and universities, these are lessons you simply can't learn in a classroom. They're learned through experiences, often tough ones.

Fortunately, Gary makes it easier by sharing his own journey to minimize the missteps in yours. His guidance was crucial to my own success in growing and selling multiple businesses, and I can never repay him for what he's given me: not just lessons but new ideas, strategic network introductions, and now, this book.

So if you're striving to realize your own entrepreneurial vision—to define it and the concrete steps you need to take, and to hold yourself accountable for following them, despite any obstacles that may arise—my advice is simple.

Read on.

Allan D. Koltin, CPA, CGMA

Allan D. Koltin is the CEO of Koltin Consulting Group Inc., a Chicago-based consulting firm. Named as one of Inside Public Accounting's "Top 10 Most Recommended Consultants," he's been inducted into both the CPA Practice Advisor's Accounting Hall of Fame and AAM's Accounting Marketing Hall of Fame. He's also been voted among the "Top 100 Most Influential In Profession" by Accounting Today for 19 straight years, and a "Top 25 Thought Leader" by CPA Practice Advisor for the past six.

PROLOGUE

If you had asked me whether I was an entrepreneur or had an entrepreneurial spirit when I first started working at my father's firm in high school in 1969, I'd have looked at you like you were crazy.

I was going to be a successful doctor.

That didn't happen, though. With my personality, good instincts, ability to see opportunities and understand how to capitalize on them, and a little luck, I became a successful entrepreneur.

This book is my way of paying it forward. The book is divided into two parts: my journey and the lessons learned along the way; and how to apply those lessons to everything you do in life and in business.

MY JOURNEY

The first eight chapters of this book describe my journey as a serial entrepreneur. I learned a lot about how businesses work—and about myself. When I started at my first "real" job at what is now Deloitte, I was a little scared. Here I was, starting at one of the top firms in the country, with no idea what to expect. I probably envisioned becoming a partner one day, which in those days was a typical dream.

Instead, it turned out to be the beginning of an incredible journey. Within a few months, I was promoted. This was unheard of back then, but I earned the promotion because I had taken the initiative to shake things up. I'm pretty sure I didn't know I had the confidence to do that when I started the job. But that's one of the things I learned—and continue to learn—about being entrepreneurial: it's a combination of seeing opportunity and knowing what to do about it.

When I was in high school, I don't remember consciously thinking of my father's firm as an entrepreneurial opportunity. When I eventually joined him, I wasn't focused on how, or even if, we would grow.

But there was a need for me to bring in enough business at his firm to pay my salary. And so, it's not an exaggeration to say that *need* changed the course of my life.

Over the next several decades I created eight separate entities. Different economic and cultural dynamics impacted how each business evolved, but that is not the whole story. The true crux of entrepreneurial success lies outside of the actual business and within the person who passionately leads its development and remains committed through the ups and downs.

As I chronicled my experiences, I realized that sharing the behind-the-scenes qualities that make up the building blocks of success could serve as a valuable resource for people who are passionate about bringing their vision to life. This led to the second half of the book, that assesses *how* to make this happen.

As you read this, keep in mind that entrepreneurs come in all shapes, sizes and ages. The forces which shape tomorrow's workforce are breeding new entrepreneurs. This trend started in the 1980s, when the long-held tradition of staying in one job for life began to fade. Today, we are seeing the results of this shift. Millennials are on the path to becoming the most entrepreneurial generation we've seen in a long time, and Generation Z has a similar outlook.

Many people, especially those who joined the workforce during the Great Recession, were not able to follow the career paths they envisioned for themselves. Jobs simply weren't available. To follow their passions—and some would say out of necessity—a new crop of entrepreneurs started their own enterprises.

Older people, too, are becoming entrepreneurial. Many Baby Boomers have a vision of retirement drastically different from the generations that came before them. For these people, the concept of retirement means mentoring or starting a charitable endeavor rather than golfing every day. They are doing things they believe in.

- If you have a vision and a strategy for seeing that vision come to life, you are on your way to becoming an entrepreneur.

- If you are passionate about seeing your vision fulfilled, you are on your way to becoming an entrepreneur.

- If you are committed to seeing the vision through, willing to be fluid and flexible as the vision moves from idea to reality, you are on your way to becoming an entrepreneur.

- If you understand you can't do it all, and are willing to put the right people in the right positions, you are on your way to becoming an entrepreneur.

- If you recognize the path will not be a straight one, and you are willing to see beyond the curves, you are on your way to becoming an entrepreneur.

- If you understand juggling priorities is part of the job description, you are on your way to becoming an entrepreneur.

- If you can accept responsibility for the buck stopping with you, you are on your way to becoming an entrepreneur.

LESSONS LEARNED

Think about how long it took when you were a kid to become frustrated trying to figure out a Rubik's Cube or learning to play a sport. How many times did you try? Did you learn how to do it from others? Did you give up after a while, or did you find yourself thinking about it when you were doing other things?

Your answers provide clues about whether you are a natural entrepreneur. There are those people whom others look at and say, "Everything he or she touches turns to gold."

Maybe they do have a magic touch, but only because they possess the right combination of traits.

Consider the popular TV show, "Shark Tank." Everyone on the program—judges and contestants—are entrepreneurs. The judges choose whether to invest in a company based on their gut feelings, which translates directly into whether they feel passionate about the product or service being pitched. Yet even the "losers" generally continue their quest for success with their products or services… and many are ultimately successful.

Other entrepreneurs succeed because they partner with someone who has complementary traits: for example, a big picture person with a detail-oriented one, or an outgoing sales person with a technical expert. These partnerships are successful because the parties recognize each other's personal strengths and weaknesses, and aren't afraid to find the right people to help fill the gaps.

For entrepreneurs, failure is not defeat. Rather, failure becomes an opportunity to learn from missteps and move forward.

The reality is that takes a lot of effort to transform your ideas into gold. The chapters in the second part of this book explain how eight of my endeavors succeeded because of those attributes entrepreneurs possess.

Part 1

MY STORY
OF BUILDING

SS&G

Chapter 1

SS&G: A LABOR OF LOVE

ACKNOWLEDGEMENTS

I would especially like to thank my partners Bob Littman and Mark Goldfarb who sat in the pilot's cabin for much of the journey. I would like to thank all my partners for believing and following me and especially those that voted to keep the dream alive.

I had the pleasure of working with hundreds if not thousands of professionals at SS&G for 33 years—my sincere thanks.

Thanks, too, to our many supportive and loyal clients, without whom we could not have been successful.

Of all the businesses and endeavors with which I've been involved, SS&G was probably the most satisfying and challenging—and certainly the one with the longest tenure. We even became a Top 40 CPA firm before we were sold in 2014 to BDO.

* * * * *

THE BACK STORY

I like to say my accounting career started around 50 years ago. In 1966, my father, Marvin, then in his mid-40s, decided to leave his job as controller for a small business to become a CPA. He signed up for the Becker CPA Review Course, which at the time was being taught by its founder, Newt Becker. During the course, he met Ted Saltz. Ted would become his partner in what would eventually be SS&G.

On November 1, 1968, Page, Saltz & Shamis opened its doors. The business consisted of Ted's small practice, made up of mainly after-market auto parts stores; my father's business, which worked with small businesses; and the practice they bought from Walter Page, who had decided to leave public accounting. Walter had been in business for many years when my father and Ted bought his firm. Because the Page name was somewhat known in the community—and he had a solid book of business they wanted to retain—it made sense to keep it.

The firm was very small. Even after acquiring Walter's clients it only employed eight people. During the firm's first busy season in 1969, I was a 10th grader at Cleveland Heights High School, which was right around the corner from their offices. After school, I went to the office and copied tax returns until dinner time, when I would go home with my Dad to eat. After dinner, Dad went back to work. We followed that routine until I graduated from high school.

After graduation, I went to Tulane University, majored in biology and daydreamed about becoming a doctor. I had a bit of an interest in accounting and wanted to take some courses. Back then, Tulane did not have a business school, so I took the only two accounting courses available through their school of continuing education.

One class, taught by Professor Paul Hooper, had only two students—including me. After I finished those two courses, I arranged for independent study with the professor. I did well in school and graduated with honors, earning a degree in biology. I also had accrued 16 credit hours of accounting.

I applied to medical school as planned but didn't get in because my boards weren't high enough. I was disappointed and wanted to reapply as soon as possible. While I was waiting to reapply, I secured a job working at a dog lab in a Cleveland hospital. My job was to help with surgery and lab experiments on dogs. The nature of this particular surgery was to induce surgical shock to dogs such that none of them survived. Not surprisingly, I hated it.

This turned out to be the luckiest thing that ever happened to me. I decided not to reapply to medical school—but I had to do something, and it wasn't going to involve dog surgery. Inevitably, I turned to the family business: accounting.

The good news was not only did I enjoy accounting, it was also a practical choice—I already had 16 credits toward a degree. By this time, most of my friends had graduated college and were working full-time. I was way behind because my undergrad degree was in biology. Another undergraduate degree didn't seem like a great idea, so I set my sights on earning a Masters of Accounting. In 1976, I enrolled at The Ohio State University.

Accounting wasn't the most popular track at OSU, but it was available and aligned with my new goal. I ended up going to school for eight straight quarters—almost three years—because it took so long to get caught up. But I persevered, and graduated first in my class.

Along the way, I even taught some accounting courses. Recruiters sat in on some of these, and as a result I received job offers from every one of the then-Big 8, as well as from what is now Grant Thornton. It was an interesting time, for sure. I had gone from having my dream of being a doctor rejected to being wildly in demand. Life sure had changed, and I ended up taking a job in late 1978 with Touche Ross (which is now Deloitte) and moved to Atlanta, Georgia.

Within six months, I was promoted to senior auditor. That, too, was amazing. It usually took two to three years to be promoted to "senior," but there was a reason for my promotion and it had a profound influence on my career: I was the only person there who could get an audit done under budget.

This was a great revelation, but it meant I didn't have enough billed hours to charge clients. So, I was in trouble for billing too few hours and a hero for getting the job done so quickly. My brain was spinning. Consider this: I could do two or three audits in the same time it took my peers to do one. We all followed the same work process. We all were smart. What was I doing differently?

I'm not sure I consciously thought about it at the time, but looking back my organizational and time management skills created efficiencies that weren't being duplicated by others. It was frustrating, and made even more so because what was a good thing in terms of productivity was viewed as a negative. After a while, I became disillusioned and realized I needed to make a change.

I wasn't sure what my next move would be, but my personal life was a major factor in the decision to move back to Cleveland. My wife Mary Ann and I (we'd married in 1979) were traveling back to visit family every chance we had—which meant we never had time to travel to other places. We were either in Cleveland or Atlanta. It became a joke between us, and we decided that moving back to Cleveland was the only way we'd get to travel to other places.

Once we knew the where I had to decide about a job. As it turned out, I was lucky because MaryAnn and I both came from accounting families, and it was likely I could easily find a position.

Another thing I had going for me was that I had passed the CPA exam before I graduated college. You can no longer do that, but at the time it was common. This meant I had the credentials I needed as I moved forward in my career.

I interviewed with both my father's firm and my father-in-law's firm, Heinick & Slavin. At the time, my father-in law's firm was the largest CPA firm in Akron, and he was the managing partner. The firm was 10 times the size of my father's firm.

This put me in a tough spot and made for a very difficult decision. At first blush, the opportunities seemed much greater at my father-in-law's firm, which had a culture similar to what I'd experienced at Touche Ross. Still, I knew my father wouldn't understand if I chose that path. Hurting him was the last thing I wanted to do. In the end, I decided to join my dad's firm, which had agreed to match what I'd been making at Touche Ross.

On August 1, 1981, I started working at Page, Saltz & Shamis. It was a huge transition—especially since it became obvious on day one that there was nothing for me to do. There were no clients for me to work on, and no program or plan in place to change that. Further, the firm's specialty was tax, not audit or assurance. I needed to learn tax accounting—quickly.

I was 28 years old, and at a loss about what to do next. These were very trying times, and I wondered whether I'd made a huge mistake. Ultimately, I decided to stay the course. There was only one thing I could do to improve my situation: go out and secure new accounts. Yet, if you asked me to list my best skills, I probably would have said I was highly organized and managed my time well. Developing business—selling—would never have made the list. No one was more surprised than I was when I soon became the firm's top rainmaker. Within six months, the firm was finally earning enough to pay my salary. It was a relief.

I was lucky to learn so much about myself early in my career. Beyond finding out I knew how to land clients, I also discovered I enjoyed being out of the office, learning what was going on with local businesses and figuring out ways to help them. I was happy.

Nothing is perfect, however. Working with my dad's partner, Ted Saltz, was toxic. Our personalities clashed. He wouldn't listen to my suggestions and thought his way was the only way. That's exactly what I didn't like about Touche Ross, and I began to think I'd jumped from the frying pan into the fire. Suddenly, my happiness turned to frustration. And, after about a year, I started seeking out alternatives. I spoke to my father-in-law about moving to Akron and inquired at Touche Ross about moving back to Atlanta. Both wanted me. I had options, which was a good thing.

Finally, I had a conversation with my dad. I explained how unhappy I was and told him I had to leave. He suggested the two of us split off and start our own practice. I was uncomfortable with that idea because he was getting older and it wouldn't have been wise for him to assume that kind of risk. I wanted to speak with Ted, but he was impossible to talk to at the office. He seemed to have two phone calls going at all times.

The upshot was that things remained status quo until one day, a couple weeks later, when I found myself alone with Ted while we were driving to see a client. I told him I had decided to leave.

He was genuinely upset.

Ted told me he understood how difficult he was to work with. We spoke at length about it. He promised to stay out of my way if I agreed to stay.

It wasn't an easy decision to make. There were many factors to weigh, both personal and professional.

On the personal side, I'd be disappointing my father-in-law a second time if I didn't join his firm. Professionally, I had to consider the opportunity for professional advancement as well as financial considerations. Lastly, I had to factor in my personal goals.

Financially, my income would be higher at Heinick & Slavin, at least initially, and I anticipated I would eventually become an audit partner. The potential at Page, Saltz & Shamis was entirely different. I'd make partner there, too, and I'd be financially OK. The difference was the job description: I would have more personal gratification because I'd be able to continue developing business, which I really enjoyed, along with doing my audit work. At the time, the firm's revenue was about $200,000 and we had about 10 employees. So, in addition to doing what I liked, I'd be able to help shape the firm to my vision of a more progressive firm.

The decision-making process was a defining experience. I did a certain amount of due diligence learning about other firms and the opportunities they had to grow. In effect, I was deciding between the status quo—paying my dues and eventually becoming a partner at an established firm—or leading a pretty small, staid firm into the future.

Ultimately, one of the factors that played into my decision was an intangible. Some time in the summer of 1982, my father-in-law asked me to accompany him to a MAP conference in Columbus. I never even knew such conferences existed. There were actually courses to teach you how to manage a CPA firm. Realizing that CPAs thought about how a firm should be run was amazing to me. I became a disciple of MAP conferences, so much so that in the late 1990s I became Chairman of the AICPA MAP Committee.

But I digress.

I thought through my decision from different perspectives. I didn't want to wind up questioning my choice. At its core, my decision wasn't about financial success. I'd have that either way. The choice was between a certain future and a less certain future I could shape. The latter prospect was exciting. My decision was made. I would stay.

The Early Years: 1981-1987
DEVELOPING A GROWTH-ORIENTED VISION AND STRATEGY

My goal in staying with Page, Saltz & Shamis was to build a high-quality firm focused on small business and the lower end of the middle market. Between 1981 and 1985, my efforts paid off and the firm started its turnaround.

I've always believed there is no need to reinvent the wheel, so I looked at what other firms were doing. There were some great firms in town to model. One was Cohen & Company, which was much larger, and is still in existence. The other was Kopperman & Wolff, which has since merged into another firm. I studied those firms, as well as my father-in-law's firm, as best I could from the outside. I analyzed what they did well, and began formulating a vision and strategy.

Hiring the right people is one of the keys to any organization's success. Today, I believe that more than ever. No one knows everything, and as the saying goes, "You don't know what you don't know." Being confident enough to hire someone who knows more than you do in a particular area is the mark of a true leader. These days, those skills might include data management, artificial intelligence or social media marketing. Back then, it was hiring staff that were better able to see the big picture and enjoyed interacting with clients.

Through my exercise, I realized the staff at Page, Saltz & Shamis wasn't the right fit for my vision. They were nice people and good accountants, but they didn't have that "extra something" I sought. As a result, I wound up firing almost everyone except for Ted, my dad, and Cindy Ambrozic—who, at the time, was a high school student. There was no reason to let Cindy go, so I kept her. She eventually became a tax accountant who stayed with the firm.

Hiring talented accountants who understood my vision became a priority. Howard Klein, my first hire, came from Ernst & Ernst to run the technical side of the practice. Bob Littman, who is my first cousin, was my second hire. He also came from Ernst. It probably took a year to get Bob to leave Ernst, but he made the leap.

I now had the core of a leadership team who understood my vision and could help implement the strategies to get there.

We began to move forward together by marketing the firm and implementing process improvements to ensure a more efficient practice. Looking back, it's hard to imagine where we started. As an example, one of the first things I did was implement a universal filing system. Before that, everyone filed according to their own individual system: finding a document in Ted's office was completely different than in my dad's office. The only way to fix it was to start over—which meant laying everything out on the floors and tables and organizing them by topic. It was a nightmare!

By 1985, we had fairly good quality staff in place, were attracting better clients, had basic policies and procedures in place, and were positioning ourselves to continue growing the firm. By the end of 1987, we had revenue of about $1 million and a staff of 15 to 20 people. I had also negotiated buy-out agreements with my dad and Ted Saltz, triggering at age 65, which was just a few years away. That was the first iteration of a succession plan of Page, Saltz & Shamis.

LESSON IN LEADERSHIP:
A PERSONAL CRISIS

My next crisis was unexpected. It came in February 1987, when Mark Goldfarb, my father-in-law's protégé at Heinick Slavin, asked to meet. Surprisingly, Mark confided he was unhappy at the firm and potentially interested in leaving to join the growing practice we had.

By then, my father-in-law had retired, so I didn't see a conflict. I was naïve, incredibly ambitious, and didn't think things through the way I should have. It was a clear instance of not knowing what I needed to know; not even enough to get expert advice from an attorney. I just trusted my gut and tried to structure a good deal based on the facts as I understood them.

Between February and April 15, 1987, over about a ten-week period, Mark and I met and crafted a plan. He would join Page Saltz & Shamis after tax season and open a small office in Akron. No problem.

I was on vacation when Mark gave notice. His managing partner's response was: "If you leave and take all these clients, how will we be able to pay Gary's father-in-law deferred compensation and retirement benefits?"

I was shocked. The next seven days were spent on the phone talking to attorneys and trying to figure out a way to make Mark's move happen.

We finally negotiated a settlement where Mark came over and brought business with him. In exchange, we made a payment to Heinick Slavin that covered my father-in-law's retirement. After much back and forth, we were able to stretch the payout period to 10 years. This allowed us to maintain the cash flow we needed over that time.

Mark and a part-time assistant opened our Akron office on May 1, 1987. It accomplished a milestone for the firm: we'd expanded our geography.

LESSON LEARNED: SELF-CONFIDENCE DOESN'T OVERCOME LACK OF EXPERIENCE

The experience was incredibly stressful, but it taught me a few hard lessons. First, I never again tried to do a deal without having other eyes on it. This was true of mergers and acquisitions that required legal guidance, as well as expansion into new industry or service lines—which needed a different kind of expertise.

In thinking back, this was when the seeds were planted for SS&G's Advisory Board. Getting input from others in and outside of your industry gives you a different perspective. That doesn't mean you must do what they say, but it lets you make decision in more of a big picture framework.

Second, this might have been an epic failure leaving Mark in a bad position at his old firm and me with a certain amount of ill-will in the local accounting community. I never again underestimated the value of good professional advice, the need to see different viewpoints, or the role tact and empathy play in negotiations.

If I could go back in time and do it again, I would do it differently. I hope I'd recognize my confidence wasn't enough to overcome my lack of experience in bringing in a lateral partner, doing a merger or negotiating with other firms. I was at a total disadvantage, in part because I wasn't prepared for things not working out the way I thought they would. I only saw one path forward, and everything on that path went my way. But that's not how the world works. Had I truly understood the value of outside advice from someone with the right expertise, I would have been more prepared for what could happen. I'd have understood there probably would be obstacles; that few paths are completely smooth. That would have made me more thoughtful in the way I moved forward and I'd have had answers ready for the "what if" scenarios that inevitably come with big decisions.

The experience was painful, but it taught me many valuable lessons. In the end, the ordeal, and it was indeed an ordeal, made me a much smarter entrepreneur.

Big Risks, Big Rewards: 1987-1999

We were very growth- and practice development-oriented, which meant we focused on growing the firm and developing a culture that encouraged staff in that direction. As a result, beginning in 1987, the firm began a period of incredibly rapid organic growth fueled primarily by some of the firm's cultural attributes. By 1995, we had 30 employees and $3 million in revenue, more than double the size we were in 1987.

BUILD IT AND THEY WILL COME

We had a problem: no more space to expand. It was a good problem, but it meant we either had to lease more space or build our own.

In 1987, we decided to build our own office building. It was a big step. We built a 10,000-square-foot building with a 5,000-square-foot basement in Solon, Ohio, about 20 miles from Cleveland. We didn't need that much space, but were optimistic enough to believe we'd grow into it.

Funny story: We still had a year on our lease when we moved into the new building. It was too short a time to sublease the space for, so we figured the amount of rent into our expenses. A couple of weeks after we moved, Sam Frankel, our landlord, called with a proposition: pay him outright for five months and he'd write off the whole year. We were thrilled. Then, shortly after we'd paid him, we found out he'd already leased the building to someone else. Lesson learned.

The space issue was more challenging in Akron. Because we rented space, there was no established infrastructure. It seemed we needed more space every time a lease came up for renewal. Eventually, in the early 1990s, we wound up building our own 9,000 square foot building. Within five years, we had to build another, bigger building. Our firm's skill in the construction and real estate industries were paramount in these endeavors, and our buildings turned into a valuable investment for our partners.

WHAT'S IN A NAME?

As we grew, in addition to our space issues, we went through several names changes. We were Page, Saltz & Shamis until 1987, when we became Saltz Shamis Klein & Goldfarb. Shortly after, Howard Klein, who had been my first hire, left the firm. It was another hard lesson, but it turned out he wasn't a good fit philosophically. We changed our name again, this time to Saltz Shamis & Goldfarb. Then, around 2000, we wanted to have a shorter name that was easier to remember so we called ourselves SS&G Financial Services to be contemporary in the marketplace. But we soon felt that name didn't really say or mean what we were trying to do, so we changed again—this time to SS&G CPAs & Advisors. That name stayed until we became part of BDO.

THERE'S ALWAYS ROOM FOR TALENTED STAFF

Hiring quality people when they are available is one of my core beliefs, and it has served me well in all my ventures.

In 1999, one of the firms I greatly admired, Kopperman & Wolff, lost their biggest client and was forced to lay off about 15 professionals. We weren't looking to hire at the time, but we interviewed every one of those people simply because they came from a firm I considered a role model. We wound up hiring five outstanding people.

Four of them still work for the firm today—two as partners and two as senior professionals. One person left a few years ago, but is still a very good friend of the firm.

INVESTING IN THE FUTURE REQUIRES PERSONAL SACRIFICE

The decisions we made around office space and additional personnel required a huge financial investment because we self-financed everything. By then, we were four partners. I remember taking a 40 percent cut in pay. My partners also took a substantial pay cut. It took about a year to return to our previous level of compensation.

I've been lucky. This was the only time in the entirety of my career that I ever went backwards in terms of compensation. Having to make that kind of sacrifice, and doing so with the innate belief that it is only a temporary setback, is something nearly all entrepreneurs face at some time in their careers.

However, that one step backwards allowed the firm to take giant steps forward. We had entered a new phase of growth, and were on a roll.

GROWING PAINS:
CINCINNATI OHIO, HERE WE COME

While I was at Touche Ross in Atlanta, I was directly involved in recruiting Ted Saltz's nephew, Brad, to the firm. We worked together at Touche Ross until I moved back to Cleveland. When Brad left Touche Ross in 1983, he left public accounting and went to a fledgling restaurant company called Houston's, whose headquarters were in Atlanta. Brad stayed at Houston's for about 12 years. He was the CFO, and by the time he left, Houston's was the most successful and admired restaurant franchise in United States.

In 1995, Brad visited Cleveland and asked to meet for lunch. It had been a while since we'd seen each other, and it was great seeing him. A few days later, he called and confided that he was considering leaving Houston's. Brad has a son with an intellectual disability and wanted to move to Cincinnati, Ohio, to get better care and services for him, as well as to be closer to family. He said he'd like to join the firm and asked if we would consider opening a Cincinnati branch office.

We saw an exciting opportunity, but this was new territory. We'd never acquired any firms or considered opening an office in another part of Ohio. We did know one thing, though: if we decided to move forward, we wanted an infrastructure we could build upon; we definitely didn't want to start from scratch.

We hired a consultant, Jay Nisberg, to help us find a firm we could merge with that would be a good fit. We stumbled on a small, 15-person Cincinnati firm named Joe Smith, CPA. We went ahead with the merger, and Brad worked there for a while.

Unfortunately, it quickly became apparent that the merger wasn't working. There were lots of reasons for this, but the most important might be that Joe simply wasn't ready to merge. He probably thought he was when we started negotiations, but he didn't have the right team in place, and he didn't want to make any changes. We had a whole different agenda: we were a growing firm looking to shake things up. It just wasn't a good match.

Although the merger failed, Brad's time there was well-spent. He picked up a client named The Great Steak & Potato Co., a fast food franchisor with franchises in malls all over the country. Our role was servicing the franchisor and providing back office accounting service to the franchisees. This work generated somewhere between $300,000 to $400,000 annually. It was the start of SS&G's highly successful restaurant niche.

Because Joe didn't have enough staff, Brad began to hire people. He built a team of six or seven people to service Great Steak & Potato, plus its franchisees.

We were in a tough spot. Our agreement with Joe had a termination clause, which was fortunate, but we had to decide what we wanted to do. By now it was the end of December and the termination clause had to be exercised by December 31st. If we went ahead with the merger, we'd be saddled with an unworkable arrangement that ultimately wouldn't benefit anyone. If we ended the arrangement, we'd have to quickly open and staff an office in Cincinnati.

On New Year's Eve, hours before the deadline, we met with our attorney and then called Joe to terminate the arrangement. Joe was as happy as we were. He quickly was back in his own practice and we opened our Cincinnati office in January 1996. We staffed it with Brad and the people he had hired. Our firm had now expanded out of Northeast Ohio.

LESSONS LEARNED

Our failed merger was an eye-opening process. The lessons we learned served us well over time, and we never again rushed into an acquisition.

In many ways, making a good merger is like making a good hire. The fit must be right professionally and culturally or it won't work. Joe simply wasn't ready to give up his autonomy, and we weren't able to read the signals. I'm not sure whether that was because we were so anxious to have a presence in Cincinnati, our naivete in these matters, or some other reason. The bottom line was we wanted different things.

Taking the risk of opening a new office in a new market paid off. The financial risks of such a move are obvious, and I'm not minimizing them, but the risks to your reputation can be even more important to consider. We were lucky with Joe because things ended fairly amicably. The lessons I learned from the misunderstanding when I hired Mark Goldfarb contributed to the relative ease of our demerger with Joe.

On the positive side, our theory that expertise matters was reinforced. I'll go into more detail about this in Chapter 14, but hiring Brad was an excellent decision. His in-house experience added depth to our already-growing restaurant practice. Our expansion to a new market was a positive move. Overall, we took a calculated risk to great success.

MARKETING GOES MAINSTREAM

The prohibitions against CPA advertising were lifted in 1978, but it took about 10 years for the practice to become mainstream. We were one of the first firms to do any kind of print advertising in a meaningful way. We used testimonials from successful, well-known clients to give us credibility and attention. Others soon began copying us. In 1996, we hired Kathy Sautters as our first marketing director. Her efforts were focused on increasingly more sophisticated marketing; business development wasn't part of her role and didn't even become a priority for the firm until years later.

NEVER UNDERESTIMATE THE POWER OF GOOD PRESS: CRAIN'S LIST

Our efforts paid off. Suddenly, we were on the verge of becoming a large firm. I became focused on being named to Crain's list of the largest regional CPA firms because I believed it would give us the name recognition we needed to move to the next level.

I was incredibly proud when we made it to the bottom of the list. (In 2010, we made it to second place and were the largest firm headquartered in Ohio. That was very satisfying.)

My instincts about the power of being on Crain's list were right. I learned that when Jeff Taussig Sr. of Taussig Graphic Supply (now part of International Paper) came to us looking for a new accountant. He told me he found us on Crain's list. He hired us and today, over 30 years later, we continue to represent the family.

WHAT MR. TAUSSIG TAUGHT ME

Mr. Taussig Sr. taught me another important lesson. He claimed he was looking for a new firm because his tax returns weren't done on time, even though all the information was submitted to his current firm either early or on time. He told us that every year he would get his return, hand-delivered, on April 15 or later. This upset him. It became his hot button issue.

Clearly, he was expecting us to be able to deliver based upon the promises we made him. And we did. I would personally pick up the tax work, take it back to our office, and be sure it was done and back to him way before April 15 deadline. We ended up with a great relationship, and I learned the value of keeping a promise.

PROCESSES, PROCEDURES AND PROMISES

Having well-defined processes in place and constantly honing them to become better and more efficient is a mantra I say in my sleep. Suggestions from anywhere in the firm need to be treated with respect. This was one of the hallmarks of our firm's culture.

The processes and procedures we had in place for busy season were stringent. It was the only way we could get to all the tax returns by the April 15 deadline. Consequently, right before busy season started, at some point in January, we send out a questionnaire to our clients along with a letter telling them we needed their information by a specific date, say March 1, so we could be sure their return could be filed on time. If the information came in after that date, we told them, we wouldn't guarantee their return would be completed on time.

Keeping my promises became another "rule" in any enterprise I led. Being honorable and transparent in business dealings is not always easy, but I've found it to be essential. When you get a new client, or start a new venture, you begin with a certain level of trust in others, and others' trust in you. It can be easy to violate that trust, and it can take an eternity to get it back—if you ever do.

Grow and Diversify: 2000-Present

STANDING UP FOR WHAT YOU BELIEVE IN

In the mid-1990s, we started to notice an industry trend: audit was becoming commoditized. The provider with the lowest cost won the work. The Big 6 recognized this and began using audit as their low-cost entry into mid-market clients. Once in, they would sell a significant amount of advisory services to these clients. The Securities and Exchange Commission (SEC), under the leadership of Arthur Leavitt, was investigating whether this created independence issues that would require companies to use different firms for tax and audit.

This went against everything the profession—and I—believed in. We maintained that a holistic relationship with smaller, mid-market type companies was incredibly important to the health of the company. For smaller businesses, it is practical and economical to access value-added services from their accounting firms. Often these firms didn't even provide audit services. Independence issues rarely arose. Any changes the SEC made regarding the separation of services at larger firms would trickle down to smaller ones.

In 2000, I was Chair of the AICPA's Managing Accounting Practice subgroup. The AICPA asked me to appear and provide testimony at the SEC's hearings on the matter. I worked closely with a D.C. law firm to prepare my statement. Then a funny thing happened. Chairman Leavitt looked at me and told me that since my entire presentation was hypothetical, it was pretty much a waste of time. I gave my testimony anyway.

The panel speaking after me was a group of individual state accountancy boards. Every one of them testified that they would push to have these same regulations on an individual state basis. Suddenly, my hypothetical situation had merit. A couple months later, the AICPA asked me to come to their national meeting to talk about my testimony. Chairman Leavitt spoke after me and, in front of 500 members of the CPA industry, he apologized and acknowledged the issue needed to be closely reviewed. I believe my testimony and train of thought had a big impact on the framework of Sarbanes-Oxley, and how it was applied several years later.

WHAT WERE THE BIG 6 DOING?

At SS&G we looked at what the Big 6 (eventually the Big 4) firms were doing. We did this because it fit with our strategy of being an industry leader. It never hurts to look at what other firms are doing, and those firms were the ones with deep pockets. They could afford to try things we couldn't—but we could adapt what we thought was valuable and make it our own. They were selling consulting services, and that sounded like a pretty good idea for us to try.

We ended up developing an extensive client service strategy. Between about 1995 to 2000 we built out the idea that clients could get many of the services they needed from us. Clients could get these services elsewhere, of course, but they now didn't have to look outside our firm.

We found most of our clients were buying pretty much anything we put in place that we thought was important. As a result, they were buying multiple ancillary services, which created tremendous growth. Our clients were serviced better, and we created a stickiness with these client relationships. If they wanted to leave us, they'd have to think twice. Oftentimes if they did leave, we found we were still doing some other service for them that they were not able to find a provider for elsewhere.

ANCILLARY SERVICES

For us, adding additional ancillary services was a breakthrough. We were offering services that enhanced our core offerings by meeting needs our clients had but didn't previously know they could get from us. We focused on six key areas: retirement, executive search, specialized tax services, payroll, wealth management and healthcare consulting.

It wasn't a slam dunk. Initially, we had to build cross-selling into the firm culture, which added another dimension to the growth-oriented philosophy our firm leaders already promoted.

Our entrepreneurial spirit allowed us to see the benefits of moving in this direction, but we didn't make the decision about which areas to pursue without taking the time to analyze the likelihood of success.

There is a distinction between being entrepreneurial and being reckless. We'd learned a lot every time we tried something new. We learned from our successes (like deciding to build our restaurant niche) as well as our failures (like our attempt to hire Mark Goldfarb without first getting good counsel). Here's the thing: every success and every failure contributes knowledge you can use to help shape a future endeavor. In any event, we started down this path early, in 1995, and in some cases before that. Many firms now do this sort of thing as a matter of course.

Our ancillary services included:

Retirement services: In about 1995 my partner, Bob Littman realized that many of our clients were looking to put retirement plans in place. We didn't do that type of work, so we sought outside vendors.

Once we realized a significant number of clients needed this service, we started looking at it differently: instead of seeing a referral opportunity, we saw a business opportunity. Bob did an excellent job leading the team that developed this business line, which turned out to be quite successful.

Executive search: Clients often ask their CPA to hire financial staff for their businesses. We thought this was something we should be good at and could be a huge benefit to our clients. We tried, but found we were neither good at it nor efficient. We also didn't understand how to price it. Efforts were duplicated because no one was overseeing who was looking to fill which position. It was frustrating because we knew we could do it better.

So, we looked at what we were doing, and determined that succeeding meant putting clear processes in place to centralize our efforts. You already know how important I think processes are. In the mid-1990s, we hired Polly Knox to be the point person. Polly spent almost 20 years with us, and when she retired Melissa White in our Columbus office took the job.

Specialized tax services: As a smaller firm, our tax services were vanilla. As we grew—and at the urging of Mark Goldfarb—we decided to build a team that could offer a broad range of specialized services. These included research and development of tax credits and cost segregation studies. We also supported niches in international tax, state and local tax, sales and use tax, and estate planning. These services integrated well with our retirement planning and wealth management offerings.

Payroll: Our payroll services division can trace its roots back to 1981, when Ted Saltz started a payroll company as an offshoot of Page Saltz & Shamis. No other firms were doing anything like that at the time, even though payroll is such a natural extension for CPA firms. Ted hired my wife, Mary Ann, who is an accountant, and a man named John Nasea, who was also an accountant, to start the company. We thought they had the right combination of skills to succeed. That company now has more than 40 employees and more than 1,200 clients. It was not part of the deal with BDO, and continues to operate as Paytime Integrated Payroll Services.

Wealth management: In 1999, we added wealth management services. It was a practice area trending across the industry. We found ourselves competing against major brokerage companies. Our goal was to provide a holistic way for our clients to find such services. The operation launch was led by Bob Littman, who had led our retirement planning effort. Bob hired Mike Heyne, who had prior experience in growing and starting wealth management companies. Mike was tasked with expanding our operations.

Mike ran the business until he retired in 2004. Carina Diamond took over as the lead. Today, we manage somewhere between $500 million and $600 million worth of assets. This business, which is a model of a successful wealth management businesses, was also not part of the deal with BDO, and continues to operate under the name SS&G Wealth Services.

Healthcare consulting: Our healthcare consulting practice also launched in 1999. We had a significant healthcare practice, and found a consulting service in Akron that seemed to mesh with the services we offered. In reality, the consulting practice was a CPA firm that did onsite practice management and helped run doctors' offices. We were fascinated by the concept and decided it fit with our diversification strategy.

We met with the owners and kicked the tires. And we liked what we saw. The business worked like this: A solo physician would start a practice and automatically become a small businessman. The doctor would hire an assistant, and the first assistant he ever hired would end up becoming the office manager. That person usually didn't have right skill set, so that's where the consultant came in. The CPA firm would provide consultants, who would become de facto office managers. They handled all aspects of running the doctor's office, including hiring and firing, receivables management and marketing, etc. Pricing was comparable to what a traditional office manager would earn, but it was a value-added proposition. We took a close look at it, but we passed because we couldn't cut a deal with the owner.

And then fate stepped in.

Soon after our meetings, the individual who owned the company had a heart attack and died. He was a young man in his early 40s, and normally, a practice like that dissipates quickly without the right succession. Because we were the last ones to look at the practice, the firm's leadership approached us again to ask if we were interested in buying the company. We were. We didn't know how to do the work. But we knew someone who did though. Tom Ferkovic was doing something similar for a big company out of New York. His company was involved with rollups of medical groups in various states across the country, and Tom was involved with the rollup in Ohio. He was the person leading the group, so we reached out to him.

I had lunch with Tom and asked if he knew anybody who might consider taking the position. He said he'd think about it.

Within hours, he called me back.

"Maybe I'm the right person for the job," he said.

We bought the practice, and hired Tom.

In many ways, developing the healthcare business paralleled the development of our restaurant vertical, except it wasn't inside the accounting firm. The trials and tribulations we encountered could fill its own book, but the endeavor was successful. Today, SS&G Healthcare is a multi-million-dollar company which grosses tens of millions of dollars, has hundreds of employees, and locations and clients all over the country. We didn't sell the company to BDO, and now it operates under a new name: Medic Management Group, LLC.

People, people, people. People are the backbone of any business. Over the years, we hired specialists in many of the areas we diversified into—and not all of them were CPAs. We sought out the best people, position-by-position, looking primarily for the ones we thought had the talent to help us meet our objectives. By the early 2000s, we had amassed a deep bench that few of our competitors could match. We looked a lot more like a global or national CPA firm than we did a local or regional one. Never underestimate the power of having the right people in place.

BE NIMBLE; BE SMART

The next big event that fundamentally changed our firm—as well as the entire accounting industry—resulted from the Enron/Arthur Andersen debacle, which gave rise to the 2002 Sarbanes Oxley Act (Sarbanes).

A simple way to think about Sarbanes is by breaking it into two pieces.

One piece is Section 404, which required all 16,000 public companies in existence at the time to develop and maintain a documented set of internal controls. This requirement, and particularly Section 404(b), mandated that a publicly-held company's auditor had to attest to and report on management's assessment of its internal controls. The penalty for not having this documented set of internal controls in place by 2006 was stiff—the CFO and CEO could go to jail for 10 years.

The second piece of Sarbanes put certain prohibitions on the ancillary work CPA firms could do for public companies. However, Sarbanes was a federal law, which meant it needed to be formally adopted by each individual state. Because of the groundwork we had laid, the states didn't adopt Sarbanes and the trickledown effect I was so afraid of when I testified before the SEC never came to pass. Instead, we got Section 404(b).

For the four years between Sarbanes' enactment and the 2006 compliance date, the entire industry received a massive boost: about 25 percent more work. And, there wasn't really an additional CPA to take it in. This forced the big firms, by then down to the Big 4, to fire its mid-market clients. Those clients, in turn, suddenly had to find auditors, so they moved to smaller firms like ours. We were delighted by this turn of events. Keep in mind, Sarbanes' work was not at all sensitive to fees because of its compliance nature and penalties. It was truly extraordinary.

By now, we had the capacity and and we wanted the work. We approached two local Big 4 offices and offered to help. Our pitch was straightforward: "We can help you. Would you like to direct the work you are conflicted on to us as opposed to having another Big 4 pick it up and try to get their foot in the door?"

It worked, and we ended up getting work from them. As a result, we could service clients larger than we'd ever thought we'd see. One, a $1 billion company, was fired with a standard letter that said, "Goodbye." Another was a $500 million manufacturer and distributor which received the same treatment. The Big 4 also stopped doing ancillary audit work for 401(k) plans, and that work came to us as well. The flow of work and quality of the work we suddenly picked up was amazing.

KEEP LOOKING AT THE BIG PICTURE; DON'T GET CAUGHT IN THE WEEDS

As we grew, we felt as though we were truly great and really smart. Mostly, we were just lucky. But the growth—including our new mindset—changed the face of our organization. Almost overnight, we became a much bigger firm with much bigger clients.

While all this was happening, we were undergoing a geographic expansion that had begun in 2000. Accounting is a cyclical business. There are busy seasons and slow seasons which vary according to the service being delivered. We realized the ability to move staff to different offices as the need arose was a good move, but we couldn't do it well because of where our offices were located. For example, Cincinnati is four hours away from Cleveland, making it difficult for staff to get back and forth in one day.

So, we decided to open an office in Columbus, roughly midway between Cleveland and Cincinnati. It was a smart move for several reasons: it would give us visibility; enable us to develop our brand throughout Ohio; and allow us to move staff as needed among offices without putting an undue burden on them. In addition, it would make us the only state-wide firm in Ohio.

We began looking for a firm to acquire, and in mid-2000 we merged with Green & Wallace, the ninth largest firm in Columbus.

We'd learned our lessons about merger from our experience with Joe Smith. This time, we were more careful when we did our due diligence. We interviewed a few firms before making any decisions. Green & Wallace seemed like a good cultural fit, was a decent size, and had a presence in the market. We gained five partners and 20 staff members. Now we had a large presence in Northeast Ohio, a fast-growing firm in Cincinnati focused on the restaurant industry, and an office in Columbus.

THE TURBO CHARGED COMPANY: THE BOOK THAT BECAME OUR ROADMAP FOR GROWTH

I'm smart enough to know I don't have all the answers. And, I recognize how important it is to know where to get the answers. All businesses that want to grow need to have this philosophy.

In 1998, I read *The Turbo Charged Company,* by Larry Goddard and David Brown (Gower Publishing Ltd., 1996). I had an epiphany. I'm not sure why, maybe because it was practical rather than theoretical, but the book resonated on a visceral level. It changed my thinking about growth strategy. Here's what I learned:

Profitability Isn't a Goal; It's a Byproduct: The book was based on interviews with senior leadership in 16 U.S. companies (eight private; eight public) about the strategies each used when building their businesses. All 16 companies were highly profitable. But what interested me most was that not one of them had profitability as a goal. Instead, each focused on running their businesses. As a result, profitability was a happy byproduct.

This concept resonated deeply with me on a visceral level. I'm not sure why, but I took this core premise very seriously. As a result, we developed a firm-wide strategy based on three attributes: growth, taking care of our clients, and taking care of our people.

It turned out to be very sound strategy. The byproduct for us was success for our owners. And, as an aside, Larry Goddard ended up becoming a partner in our firm.

Strategic Competitive Advantage: The book also discussed an attribute dubbed "strategic competitive advantage." This related to owning a niche, an industry focus, or a service focus. Essentially, a strategic competitive advantage is something that gives a company a credible advantage in the business world. We began to focus significantly on our top five niches: restaurants, not-for-profits, real estate, pharmacy, and manufacturing and distribution.

MANAGING PARTNER AS CEO

By now, we had about $12 million in annual revenue, and the firm was growing quickly. It was a busy time—we had Sarbanes work, were integrating the Columbus merger, and developing our ancillary services. I was involved with everything at some level, which limited the amount of time I had to devote to my clients. Something had to change.

The Executive Committee considered the issue, and decided the firm needed a new governance structure. Because of their review, I transitioned to the position of CEO. In this new role, I no longer had direct client responsibilities. All my attention was focused on SS&G.

This transition was very unusual, especially at the time. It was strange for me as well, in some ways, especially because I truly liked working with clients. But, the shift to pure firm management nudged the firm's growth strategy into high gear.

I led the firm for 27 wonderful years, but part of the managing partner's function is having a succession plan. Mandatory retirement at the firm was at age 65. I was 60 when I stepped down. Part of my new role was guiding the new managing partner, now acting as the CEO, and assisting with the transition. I don't believe anyone is truly ready to lead a firm until they start doing it. There are many aspects to the position no one tells you about, and it isn't an easy job. For one thing, it can be lonely at the top. The managing partner is the firm's ultimate decision maker, and that can be a pretty weighty job. For another, you can be friendly with the partners who used to be your peers, but there is a subtle difference in the balance of power. Being the head cheerleader for a strong company culture is another aspect of the position. But the biggest change is that you must relinquish working directly with clients, which is a very enjoyable part of the job for many.

Managing this kind of transition teaches you a lot about yourself. The biggest lesson I learned was that I wanted to continue doing new things. So, when I eventually left the firm in 2016, I formed another company, Winding River Consulting, which I'll talk about in Chapter 8.

SS&G'S ADVISORY BOARD

Keep an Open Mind; Good Guidance Can Come from Outside Your Industry: In 1999, at the same time I became CEO, we created an advisory board. It's common practice across many industries, and we often advocated for our clients to have them. Somehow, though, the concept never resonated in the accounting industry. Instead, firms got advice from the outside consultants they brought in on a regular basis. Usually, a different person would come in each year. The consultants were good, but because they rotated so frequently they never developed a real feel for the firm or its culture.

I knew the consulting world well because I consulted on a regular basis with firms all over the country. I did this for two reasons: it was fun and I was good at it. Consulting allowed me to see first-hand how other practices operated, and I was always open to new ideas that could benefit SS&G. Because of this, I began to think an outside advisory board was the way to go. So, we decided to try it.

For SS&G's purposes, we wanted a mix of consultants in the accounting industry, successful business people, and professionals outside the accounting industry—such as lawyers and insurance professional. Essentially, we picked advisors we thought could advance our efforts. Our first advisory board consisted of three professionals: one from accounting, one from the legal industry, and a businessman. We told them the board would rotate, and that meetings would be held as needed. They were paid $2,500 per meeting, plus expenses.

Over the years, we rotated people off the advisory board based upon our need. So, if we felt that we had issues with marketing, we might have a marketing professional on the board for a few years. If we wanted to get a closer glimpse of the accounting industry, we would include someone from our industry.

Advisory board members were involved with making high-level decisions. We followed an agenda compiled with input from the board and the Executive Committee. Often, we invited guests. For example, our head of internal technology would talk about technology strategy, we would talk about growth strategy, and we'd bring in members of the firm to add to the discussion about where we were going.

At the onset, the board met annually with our Executive Committee. But we soon found the meetings were creating so much value that we started scheduling semi-annual meetings. Each meeting cost between $8,000 and $9,000. Two meeting per year would cost between $16,000 and $18,000—an amount that was more than offset by what we would have paid a consultant if we had continued with that strategy.

Although there still aren't many firms that have outside board, I strongly believe it is a sound business practice and encourage firms to think about implementing one.

TWO BOARDS MEMBERS WHO INFLUENCED MY THINKING

There were two board members who had a profound influence on my thinking: Dick Pogue, a former managing partner of Jones Day; and Rebecca Ryan, a visionary who is always looking ahead.

Dick was at Jones Day as it evolved from an Ohio firm to a national firm. He was a treasure chest of information on how to grow a firm. The two most outstanding pieces of advice he offered were: (1) to be successful at the goal level, you need to operate at a level that ensures each partner does what she or he is best at; and (2) when you open a new office, always move someone who knows the firm culture to lead the effort.

Great advice, to be sure. But the problem was even though I knew it made good policy, I didn't always follow it. When we acquired Green & Wallace in 2000, for example, we thought the transition would be smooth even if we didn't move an SS&G "home base" partner to Columbus.

We were wrong.

Between 2000 and 2005, we struggled with leadership, profitability and culture. Finally, in 2005, we moved Mike Voinovich from Cleveland to Columbus to lead the office and transition our culture. Within a short time, the office met our expectations. I'm not sure why we didn't do that initially. But here's the caveat: If someone you look to for advice makes a suggestion, at least keep their counsel in mind as you make decisions. We were lucky things went as well as they did before we took a step back and reconsidered Dick's suggestion.

Rebecca Ryan is another board member who helped us immensely. Not only did she teach us how to create a firm culture that would attract millennials, she gave me two recommendations that I use to this day.

Her first recommendation concerns capacity. The analogy she used is a visual that made me aware of the limitations of time as well as my own capacity: How many things can one person successfully manage at one time? Rebecca said, "Think of a glove as the time you have available for life and work. Once the glove is full, you can only add something if you remove something else. The only way to do that is to delegate; the power of delegating lies in the ability of the person you delegate to."

Rebecca also taught me that leaders sometimes need to do things they don't want to do—uncomfortable things, like letting people go or reversing a merger. It's inevitable these types of events will occur in one's career. When they do, they should be done with class. Always keep in mind you're not the only person who is anxious—but you are the one in charge of the situation.

FUTURE FORWARD

When I first met Rebecca Ryan (I'll offer more about her in Chapter 6), but here it's enough to say I was completely taken with her ideas for making companies and localities places where young people wanted to be. Young people are the future, and I wanted to bring her in to talk about how we could be one of those places.

We hired Rebecca full-time, and she spent one year with us. Together, we spent a tremendous amount of time focusing on how to position ourselves to be the employer of the next generation.

While we were already doing a lot of the right things, we worked with her to reinforce our efforts in areas like way our offices looked, how we used technology, our dress code, and giving frequent feedback. Rebecca developed methods for measuring how the companies she was working with were doing. She surveyed people to get their input and suggested strategic initiatives for moving forward, such as giving regular feedback, whether positive or negative—a policy particularly valued by the millennial cohort on our team.

Our efforts were rewarded.

In 2014, Vault.com ranked us No. 1 in the country for opportunities for women and No. 2 in terms of providing diversity to others within the profession. This was quite an honor, considering we were a regional firm.

THE GREAT RECESSION OF 2008

Our next real challenge came in 2008 with the arrival of The Great Recession. We had never experienced a period where we had not grown, but this felt different. We weren't sure what would happen, so we huddled and strategized about how to move forward as an organization.

We made difficult decisions, not because we wanted to, but because we believed they would be for the ultimate good of the firm. We talked about how it might be time for some of our older partners to leave and retire. We facilitated graceful exits from the firm for such colleagues. We focused on the entire firm and analyzed how we could keep our core together. We forced reductions in hours worked, lowered compensation, and found other ways for our employees to give dollars back to the firm by working less. In the end, we stayed mostly intact.

This was a new way of doing business. Up until then, we had never focused on the negative. Our efforts paid off. Within a year, we were able to turn it around. And, a few years later, we were much further ahead of where we were in 2008. Because of this, we began actively considering expanding to new areas of the country, and generally feeling that we had returned to business as usual.

NOT A LOT OF SECRETS

To move forward, and grow the way one wants to grow, firms need to take the time to develop a vision and a strategy that lays out a roadmap for the future. There isn't room for a lot of secrets. Everyone has access to the same information. The difference lies in execution. And while this sounds so simple, it's very hard. The number of professional service firms that can execute their plans well is small. An important reason is Rebecca's glove analogy: you need capacity to execute. If the managing partner's time is largely spent on client work, he or she won't be able to oversee the execution of the firm's growth plan. Therefore, it becomes a matter of measuring the value of growing the firm against the amount of time the firm leader must devote to that goal. At SS&G, the decision was that I would be a more like a corporate CEO than a traditional managing partner.

SIDE EFFECTS: A DEEP DIVE INTO OUR GROWTH STRATEGY

The recession forced us to realize we were stymied in terms of growing in Ohio. We already were the largest firm headquartered in the state, so we started looking at how we could grow outside of our core marketplace. We identified four or five cities we felt would be good fit based upon several different demographics: Was it easy to get there? Was there opportunity? Were there any potential merger partners in one of our niche areas? Here's what we found:

Chicago: After much thought, we chose to focus on Chicago first. We'd never done a merger outside of Ohio, and we thought another Midwestern city would be a good start. The consensus was they would speak the same language and have the same values as we did. Also, although we had an amazing restaurant practice, we weren't in any of the great restaurant cities. Chicago is a one of those cities, and we already had many clients there.

It was a good decision. Between 2010 and 2014, we ended up consummating three mergers in Chicago: a firm in Des Plaines; one in the downtown area of River North; and a third in Skokie. When the dust settled, we had about 100 people in Chicago, along with a significant restaurant practice. Practically, overnight, we became the 20th largest firm in Chicago.

New York City: New York City was the other market we were interested in, mostly due to the restaurant practice. I interviewed about a half-dozen firms over a few years' time, but never found the right fit.

I had a friend in New York named Dana Zukofsky. Dana and I had met in 2008, when she was terminated from another CPA firm. She reached out to me through LinkedIn in search of opportunities. I really liked her, and after we had failed at trying to find a firm in New York, I asked if she had any interest in joining us.

She declined.

Six months later, she had a change of heart and was willing to consider it. We flew her to a restaurant conference in Las Vegas to meet the rest of our restaurant team. Everything clicked. Before she left the conference in Vegas, we had put together a deal for her to start as our one-person New York office. We weren't sure how we were going to get her office space, or even how we were going to give her the tools to accomplish what we needed her to, but we were all-in. There were only two things we did know: we'd have to service the work out of other offices while we built the practice, and we wanted it to work.

I approached Jim Ellis, a contact at Capital Spring, New York's largest private equity firm within the restaurant space. We'd done quite a bit of business together, and I asked Jim about renting some space from him.

Jim said he would be happy to have Dana move into their offices, but with a caveat: he would not allow us to pay for the space.

That's how Dana wound up sitting in the middle of 40 private equity representatives who were working with restaurant clients.

It seemed as if every day, someone walked up to Dana and asked her to work with their clients. We grew fast, and soon hired someone to work with her. That was in the fall of 2014, just before we announced we were going to be joining BDO. The gentleman we hired moved into the BDO office, and Dana took a business development role with BDO.

Atlanta: Even as we were having merger discussions with BDO, we were in serious talks to merge in an Atlanta firm. That firm eventually merged with Warren Averett instead of us.

MY PROUDEST MOMENT

My family means everything to me. I'm very proud of them. I'm also proud of my accomplishments as a businessman and a good citizen. One of my proudest moments came when these worlds met through my daughter, Melissa.

When Melissa was a senior at the University of Michigan, she entered the Ross School of Business's Entrepreneurship Challenge. She and her team elected to open a restaurant in Seattle. Part of the reason was that Melissa, who was team leader, thought I could help with things like reviewing projections. Her team did a lot of research before they started their project.

Unbeknownst to me, part of the research included a meeting Melissa's professor set up with the two owners of Zingerman's in Ann Arbor. Zingerman's is a famous U.S. franchise with a renowned culture.

Melissa was well prepared for the meeting—dressed in a business suit and with a list of questions. The interview went very well. And then, Melissa asked one last question: "Who is your CPA firm?"

The duo responded they used a firm in Detroit. To which Melissa countered, "You should use SS&G. They specialize in companies like yours." And then she handed them a few pages she had printed off our website.

A short while later, she texted me: "Dad, I just opened the door at Zingerman's. It's up to you to close it."

On one hand, I was blown away. On the other, I was worried she'd been too aggressive. I emailed Paul Saginaw, one of the owners, and apologized if my daughter had acted inappropriately. This started an exchange, and I wound up inviting Paul and his CFO to our restaurant boot camp in Las Vegas.

The group of us had dinner the night before the boot camp. And, within a year, Zingerman's became a client. Melissa got a referral fee through SS&G's Cash-for-Clients program.

BDO: A NEW NAME; A NEW WAY FORWARD

Eighteen months after I stepped down as CEO, SS&G became part of BDO. I didn't anticipate this would be SS&G's next chapter. In retrospect, I should have. But I was so focused on growing the firm that I didn't fully realize how sought after we were in an industry undergoing major consolidation.

Over the years, we'd been courted by many large firms. We spoke to all of them to learn why we were such an attractive target. And, we had another motive: to learn what they were doing, too.

Even though we had become the 37th largest CPA firm in the country and had $80 million in revenue, our brand was a local one. It wasn't recognized across the country. We saw evidence of this with two long-time clients that had grown up with our firm and become household names. We lost them both—and not because of the quality of our work.

Both organizations were up-and-comers in the restaurant space, with huge up-side potential, when we began working with them. Both attracted private equity, and perhaps even venture capital, to spur their growth. Both were headed toward public offerings.

Within a very short period, the private equity firm removed us from all the assurance work. The SS&G name simply wasn't known to individual investors, so it didn't have the credibility they required.

We thought about this while we entertained discussions with other Top 100 firms in the middle of the pack. None of them offered us a larger a brand than we already had. That's not to say that these firms weren't, and aren't, great firms. We just could not see how we would be better off unless we merged with a nationally—if not internationally—recognized brand. That left the Big 4, BDO (No. 5), Grant Thornton (No. 6), and RSM (No. 7) as the logical candidates for us to merge with. We were approached by four of these seven firms.

Of them, BDO was only one without an Ohio presence. Joining them seemed to make the most sense. Also, BDO provided a deal far superior to any of the deals we had seen from anybody else.

Another, more personal consideration came into play as well: Wayne Berson, CEO of BDO, and I had been friends for nearly 20 years. We respected each other, independent of the merger, and with that came a certain degree of comfort.

Nevertheless, the decision to move forward was very difficult.

We spent more than two months in internal discussions about the opportunity, and had numerous meetings with BDO. Finally, in October 2014, a super majority of our partners voted in favor of going forward with the merger. The deal closed January 1, 2015.

RESTAURANT CFO
BOOTCAMP®

Chapter 2

BUILDING A NICHE

ACKNOWLEDGEMENTS

Our restaurant vertical couldn't have happened without the help of Brad Saltz, Adam Berebitsky, Lisa Haffer, Alexis Becker, Dirk Ahlbeck, Mike Perlman, Dustin Minton, Ilana Isakov-Katz, Kate Blakemore, and Dana Zukofsky.

* * * * *

In 1981, when I started working at my father's firm, I immediately realized there was no work for me and no plan for how to pay my salary. I was stunned, and wondered what I had gotten myself into. It didn't take very long for me to figure out that I'd have to earn my own salary. That is, I'd have to bring in enough business for the firm to pay me.

This was a true wake-up call. I had little idea how to attract business; the so-called soft skills weren't in the curriculum back then, and there was no one at the firm who could mentor me.

I learned by doing, and found I had a knack for being a rainmaker. Rainmaking probably is the skill that was most important in shaping my future, but it wasn't the only one. Entrepreneurs have a bundle of skills; each is core to the business' success, yet each can be delegated to some degree.

One of my first accounts was Tom Lutz, the owner of the former Gamekeeper's Taverne in Chagrin Falls, Ohio. Tom was different than our typical clients. He was personable. He had a service mentality. He was exciting. And, he definitely wasn't formal. I enjoyed working with him so much so that I serviced his business until it closed in spring of 2017. Tom and I became such good friends that I became part-owner of the restaurant—not something you would expect to happen from an accountant-client relationship!

Tom was my first restaurant client. As I was putting together my own book of business I wondered, "Why can't all clients be as much fun?"

Restaurant clients became my focus. By 1995, I was working with 20 restaurants. That year, when Brad Saltz moved back to Cincinnati and joined the firm, I knew we had something special. Because he had been CFO of Houston's, Brad's knowledge of the restaurant industry came from the inside. His 12-year-stint was from an entirely different perspective from mine, and it was a good balance. It allowed us to get a full picture of our clients: how they managed; where they could improve their processes; what internal controls were in place. Our ability to look at our clients' operations from both sides allowed us to spot where they could make improvements. We thought this put us in a great position to market to the restaurant industry. And, we believed the adage: If you build it they will come.

But they didn't.

After an early success getting the Great Steaks franchise as a client when we first opened our Cincinnati office, we grew very slowly. Great Steaks chose us primarily because of Brad's success at Houston's, but nobody else came knocking on our door. It took until the early 2000s to grow the practice from $50,000 to about $1 million—not exactly what we had envisioned. We decided we needed a more targeted strategy to achieve our goals… and dominate the niche.

DEVELOPING A GROWTH STRATEGY

The U.S. restaurant industry is enormous. It doesn't have many large publicly-held companies, but it does have a lot of large restaurant groups. Only the federal government employs more people. It's a volatile industry, though, with a high failure rate. And, because it is considered a cash business, many CPA firms choose to stay away from it.

The restaurant industry also is segmented. We understood that, and decided we did not want to service all areas. Our target market was large, sophisticated privately-held groups, franchisors, and large franchisees. Our typical client had annual revenue between $25 million and $100 million, multiple state and city issues, a large number of employees, and concerns about finance and structure.

We did many good things for our clients, and they were happy with our work. We saw unlimited opportunities in the sector—but we had to figure out how to harness and make it work for us.

A SHIFT IN THINKING:
FROM "COME FIND US" TO "HERE WE ARE"

My goal was clear: make SS&G a go-to firm for large restaurant groups and franchisors. The issue was figuring out the differentiators: What was the hook we could use to get people in the industry to start noticing us? Who were our biggest competitors and why were we better?

I shifted my thinking from "come find us" to "here we are." That required research. It was a process. My sources were the then-fledgling Internet, as well as numerous other available vehicles. For example, I went to the AICPA's national restaurant conference and got a list of the participants. I traced them back to their firms and then looked for whatever information I could find on the firms. I searched the Internet for things like "restaurant CPAs."

In the end, there were only three firms besides SS&G—and the Big 4—with a national restaurant practice: J.H. Cohen in New Jersey (now CohenReznick), Blackman Kallick in Chicago (now part of Plante Moran), and HORNE LLP in Jackson, Mississippi.

A deeper dive revealed that J.H. Cohen's restaurant niche didn't service anybody outside of New York City; Blackman Kallick's practice was built around one large client and focused on the Chicago market; and HORNE did mostly restaurant bookkeeping rather than traditional restaurant work. There was definitely an opening for us.

We already had most of the significant restaurant business in Ohio, and believed we could dominate the market because of our expertise. We recognized we'd have to compete on a national level. The next step was formulating a strategy to make the market aware of our firm and its capabilities. This required us to answer two related questions: How do we market to national clients? And how do we build capacity to service them?

The former led us to realize our marketing efforts were successful using traditional methods in our local market. But, we needed to develop a separate and different marketing strategy to compete on a national level.

The latter question wasn't anything new. It was a classic problem for any growing company. For us, however, the dilemma was whether to get the work and then hire... or vice versa.

MARKETING DIFFERENTLY AND WITH PURPOSE

The solution we landed on was one we believed would work for us now, and position us for future growth. We built a sophisticated marketing plan that turned out to be a constant work in process—a framework that is continually upgraded, redefined, and honed. Our comprehensive strategy had eight components:

Thought leadership. Positioning ourselves as thought leaders in the restaurant industry was an important component of our plan. We spoke at restaurant industry events as well as accounting industry conferences. We also published our *Selections* newsletter (see below), which had a wide readership.

We used our thought leadership program in this niche, as well as in others, as a great way to present our next generation leaders to our clients as well-regarded specialists. We forced our young leaders to step out of their comfort zones and take responsibility at a high level very quickly. It's very rewarding to nurture young leaders and watch them develop this way.

We also positioned ourselves as thought leaders by developing an industry newsletter called *Selections*. It was a graphically appealing six-page newsletter containing industry-specific articles related to accounting, finance, taxation and personnel matters. We kept it light-hearted and often highlighted clients that were doing cool things. Thousands of people ultimately were on our mailing list. (As times changed, *Selections* evolved into a blog.)

Industry-specific newsletters like this have a long shelf life. As we intended, people started associating our name with restaurant accounting.

Through the years, numerous CPA firms asked to buy subscriptions to the newsletter, but that wasn't in our plan. We didn't want to be publishers.

We wanted the newsletter to remain proprietary because it showcased that we were on the cutting edge of a highly competitive industry. Our name was a recognizable brand across our target segment of the industry, which became our goal.

This decision epitomizes the definition of a good entrepreneur. We took advantage of many opportunities when they presented themselves— hiring Brad for his restaurant experience, for instance, or starting ancillary businesses that grew out of our clients' needs—but becoming a publisher was different. It was starting an entirely new business that had nothing to do with SS&G's vision and mission.

This isn't an assessment of whether we would or wouldn't have been successful. It's merely a statement about the importance of knowing where you want your business to go and grow, and not deviating from that. Build on it, yes, as we did. Going entirely off course, no. That's counterproductive.

If we had decided to become publishers, it would have been as an entirely new entity staffed by experts in that area. We would have a stake in the business and might have acted as advisor, but we would not have actively worked in the business or formed it as an ancillary enterprise. The SS&G brand would not have been associated with it in any way.

Advertising. Because national advertising platforms as so expensive, we were careful about where we spent our money. Since our business focused mostly on restaurant finance and restaurant franchisees, we chose *Restaurant Franchise Times* as our primary platform. Its subscribers were closely aligned with our target audience. We published advertorials written around technical, tax or industry-specific information. It turned out to be a good choice that brought us clients.

Industry conferences. We'd always gone to accounting conferences focused on the restaurant industry. They were interesting and informative on lots of levels, but they didn't help us get new clients.

We thought about that a lot and finally had an epiphany: we wouldn't find new clients by meeting with other accountants, we could only do that by being with restauranteurs. That meant we had to change direction and become involved in restaurant industry conferences. It was a huge transition centered on getting clients. We were mingling with clients and potential clients and hearing what they needed and wanted from us. It was a different kind of learning than what we experienced at accounting conferences.

Our first industry conference, the 2001 Restaurant Finance and Development Conference, was a revelation. There I was, in a room with 1,600 prospective new clients, and virtually no competition. It was a potential goldmine.

After that first time, we put a lot of preparation into figuring out who would be there and who we wanted to meet. That conference became our most significant networking event. The difference now is there are 20 other firms at the event.

We went to other industry conferences as well, and it was always the same. We were the first ones there and other firms followed our lead.

Of course, we still went to AICPA conferences and talked to other accountants, but that route was for our professional betterment. The industry conferences had a whole other purpose supported by our marketing professionals.

We weren't afraid to lead the way in marketing our restaurant niche, but we did it thoughtfully. We committed a lot of time and money to preparing for each conference, right down to defining our ideal client and arranging introductions to key people. The risk was worth the investment, but we were strategic about how we went about breaking the marketing mold.

Restaurant CFO Bootcamp. Our boot camp has been in existence for more than 15 years. We conducted two or three events each year. The three-day event is open to all financial professionals in the restaurant industry. The number of attendees is limited to about 60, combined. This serves the dual purpose of maintaining a sense of exclusivity and allowing the maximum possible amount of networking time. All attendees pay a fee, but the fee is discounted for clients and for multiple people per company.

Conference sessions delve into topics like benchmarking, technologies, internal controls, tax issues, and employment law. As a highlight, we usually bring in a famous restauranteur to tell their story. We've featured people from Zingerman's, Lettuce Entertain You and Cameron Mitchell, to name a few.

During the networking sessions, clients are seated with non-clients. Our clients are the ones who sell us as these groups chat informally about what they've learned. It is subtle approach, but it has worked well. These meetings serve as a window on what they are seeing on the ground.

Listen to Your Instincts. As a leader, as an entrepreneur, it's important to listen to your inner voice. Your gut will generally give you good advice. For me, getting input from outside the circle of who we're directly working with is one of those things. It permeated SS&G in many ways, from the formation of SS&G's Advisory Board to viscerally understanding how important Brad could be to our restaurant niche, to being able to accurately read what Mr. Taussig was looking for in his new CPA firm. I felt these things, and others like them, in my gut, and I went with my instincts. I can't say I was always right, but my gut feelings were 95 percent accurate across all my endeavors. Most successful entrepreneurs have the same kind of internal radar.

Benchmarking Study. One of our more innovative marketing initiatives is an annual benchmarking study where we gather data from our clients. We started publishing these reports well over 10 years ago, and they've become widely used to benchmark industry trends.

Kate Blakemore, a member of our marketing team, is dedicated to developing and maintaining the study. We purposely assigned a point person to this task to encourage relationship building with the restaurant community. Cultivating these relationships helped ensure we were monitoring the things our clients cared about. Part of this meant the survey changes every year. In addition to certain set questions (mostly demographic), the data points we discover the market wants to know about are included in our study. For example, questions about specific ROI targets or the return of assets draw interest because they're outside the customary data points respondents expect.

Changing things up is how the survey maintains its currency and relevance. It was and is a labor-intensive task. But it also provided insight to how our growth culture worked to our advantage. What we learned at boot camp fed the survey and allowed us to ask targeted and topical questions, which in turn created interest in SS&G and how it could benefit clients and potential clients alike.

Database management. Database management is a critical part of every marketing initiative, whatever it is you are selling. Having an up-to-date database shows, among other things, that you're on top of the industry to which you're marketing. I cannot stress enough how difficult this is to do.

In the restaurant industry, for example, it's common for CFOs to move from restaurant to restaurant, which makes it hard to ensure the correct name is associated with the specific position being targeted. Maintaining an up-to-date database allowed us to follow our list of CFOs as they progressed in their careers, as well as maintain personal relationships as they changed jobs.

Having a dedicated person in place to monitor these types of changes in one of our major niche areas helped a lot, but it wasn't always perfect. And it's impossible for most businesses to expend these types of resources across all business lines. Being aware of where most business is coming from—whether that's determined by client size, service area or industry segment—is key to deciding where resources should be allocated. That's stating the obvious, but there's another part to it: doing this kind of research may uncover an opportunity for expansion based on client need.

Internal Education. Internal education is a critical for any business. Our internal education program had two prongs. The first was keeping current with developments about tax and accounting matters. That's pretty much a given. We'd be abrogating our duties if we didn't do it. The second part of our effort was knowledge transfer. This is a conundrum throughout industry, as leadership transitions from one generation to the next, and even as people move from job to job.

SS&G recognized the second prong—knowledge transfer—in many ways, from my mentoring our next managing partner to continuously imparting knowledge in specific industries and service lines.

In our restaurant niche, we hold an annual retreat focused exclusively on the industry. It is during this retreat that much of the knowledge—of clients, techniques and tactics—is passed among professionals. These are the things that often are missed: What is the client's preferred method of communication? Is the client particularly sensitive to anything? (Remember Mr. Taussig, Sr., who became our client because his returns weren't always done in a timely manner by his previous firm?)

At its core, accounting is a relationship business. Most businesses are. That is why it is so critical to understand that Client A hates the color red while Client B never eats chocolate. These are personal preferences that may seem trivial on their face and aren't always mentioned, yet knowing about them can make a huge difference to a relationship. We make a great effort to be sure this type of information is memorialized.

Even with all its complexity, I believe our plan ended up being the key to our success. When we sold to BDO, the restaurant business was a $12 million niche—with 400 clients and an annualized growth rate of between 15 percent and 20 percent. We continue to evaluate new ways we can enhance its growth.

The key lesson is this: Building a niche parallels building a business. Each takes the same amount of entrepreneurial skill.

leading **edge** alliance

innovation • quality • excellence

Chapter 3

THE STORY OF THE LEA

ACKNOWLEDGEMENTS

Who would have ever believed The Leading Edge Alliance (LEA). An idea in 1999—today one of the larger associations of CPA firms in the world.

Karen Kehl-Rose was a rock-star. Dick Kretz and Bob Hottman provided the start.

Jeff Weiner, Mike Newton, Mike Cain, Carl Barranco, and Michael Davis made it happen.

* * * * *

Big firms have always had the bandwidth to service multi-state and multi-national clients. In the 1980s, as companies began looking in earnest for better, more appropriate and more economical ways to lower their tax rates and manufacturing costs, CPA firms began to understand the value of having a wider reach. They recognized that forming alliances was the best way to achieve this and still maintain their independence. These alliances became formal associations of like-minded firms that gave members the ability to work in other cities and countries without having to send their own staff to do the work. The strategy was a cost-effective strategy for making individual firms seem larger and deeper than they were.

We didn't even think about joining an association until about 1990. At the time, we had about $2 million in business and about 15 to 20 employees. By then, we were targeting larger clients and the idea of being seen as a larger firm was attractive. We interviewed a few associations and decided on one we thought had what we needed, so we joined.

As it turned out, it wasn't a good fit. That failure was the beginning of a journey into what became one of my proudest accomplishments.

DON'T EVEN TRY TO BE SOMETHING YOU AREN'T

Once I got involved in the association and began to understand how it worked, I made some suggestions about how to improve the association from a member's perspective. If you are one of the lucky people with the ability to build businesses, you'll find that trying to adapt and improve processes and procedures comes naturally. The specific setting isn't necessarily relevant. It just doesn't sit well if you find yourself in a situation where your views aren't at least listened to because even if your ideas need to be tweaked or ultimately aren't adopted, there usually is something worth exploring.

A RUN-IN WITH THE RULES

Things seemed to be moving in a positive direction at the association. Then I went to a meeting in Phoenix in 1995, and everything changed.

The meeting was held right around the time Brad Saltz was preparing to join us and we were planning to open a Cincinnati office. I brought Brad, who would essentially be the only employee in that office, to the meeting so he could meet everyone. We knew there was already a well-established Cincinnati firm in the organization, but we didn't see any conflict.

Most associations have a managing partners-only session as part of their conference, and this one was no different. The session allows managing partners to discuss issues that concern them with their peers in a collegial environment.

The session was going well when, late in the afternoon, the conference chair asked me to leave the room so they could discuss the "issue."

I had no idea what he was talking about, but I left the room under protest. I was totally blindsided.

Jay Nisberg, who was, ironically, the consultant I'd used to help with establishing a Cincinnati office, was a speaker at the conference. He happened to be sitting outside the room, and we sat together until the meeting broke up.

After the meeting ended and people started filing out of the room, I felt like I was in the Twilight Zone. No one looked at me; no one spoke to me.

There was a networking event that evening, and Brad and I planned to attend. We were sitting on the porch of our casita (everyone had a casita as their hotel room) talking before going to the event. Soon other attendees began passing us on their way to the event. No one looked at us or stopped to speak. It was surreal.

Then one partner stopped in front of us. He said, "I'm sorry you were thrown out of the association."

What?!

Well, it turns out the association had a rule mandating geographic exclusivity. Two member firms couldn't operate in the same market. We violated the rule because we were opening an office in Cincinnati.

I had never seen the by-laws and, in any case, I thought the rule was nonsense. We were never officially notified that we were no longer members of the association, or anything else for that matter. No one on the association's leadership team would even take a phone call from me. I was incredibly angry.

Only one individual, a gentleman named Leon Janks from the association's Los Angeles firm, was supportive. He helped us understand the situation and, since no one would speak with us directly, he worked with us as our liaison to resolve the issue.

BE PROACTIVE: THE BEST ANSWER MAY BE BUILDING IT YOURSELF

After that miserable experience, we tried a different association. But we weren't particularly happy there. Bob Littman took on the role of representing SS&G at association meetings. After about a year, Bob asked me to present. I did, and became convinced that the association wasn't a good fit. The other member firms weren't sophisticated enough for us to learn from. We needed an association that could make us a better firm in all areas—from technical expertise to practice management.

You know what they say, two strikes and you're out. By this time, it's was the late 1990s and we decided not to even try to look for another association to join. Instead, we realized that forming our own association was our best option.

We sought out progressive firms like ours; firms with similar beliefs about how to succeed in a rapidly changing world. Computers, mobile and the Internet were fast becoming part of the business landscape. We knew these developments were only the beginning. We wanted to be aligned with firms that could identify trends and be nimble enough to use them to their advantage. I became proactive about finding a solution to our problem. It felt good.

Research was the logical first step.

I reached out to two colleagues, Dick Kretz, from Connecticut; and Bob Hottman, from Denver, to brainstorm what elements they wanted in a premier association. I was trying to validate my hypothesis about what an association should be and what it should offer its member firms. Confirming that Dick and Bob agreed that my vision was doable was reassuring. Both were part of other associations, so they had access to firms that aligned with ours. The two of them were instrumental in attracting top firms to what became The Leading Edge Alliance.

TIMING MAY NOT BE EVERYTHING, BUT IT COUNTS

My timing couldn't have been better. Existing associations were entering their maturity, and the cream had risen to the top. Two or three larger, more forward-thinking firms were the foundation of each of these organizations, and those were the firms we decided to target as we formed LEA. Our thinking was that since these firms were progressive, they would entertain the idea of being part of a new association whose goal was leading the way for accounting firms in all areas affecting their growth and profitability.

FUNDING OUR NEW ASSOCIATION

We ended up with about 15 firms that were interested in having further discussions about our idea. Each of them contributed $5,000 to fund what was essentially a think tank.

With the $75,000 in seed money, I hired Anita Meola, who had been with the AICPA, to help write the by-laws, name the new entity, delineate the strategy, and assist in finding an executive director. Karen Kehl-Rose, who came from the Illinois Society of CPAs, was the person we hired. (She's still there.)

By August 1999, we invited all 15 firms to meet at the Ritz-Carlton Hotel in Cleveland to get to know each other and talk about our new association. We gave the firms until the end of September to let us know whether they wanted to move forward.

Initial dues were $7,500. We used the money we collected to fund Karen's salary and begin the LEA. I was the chair for the first nine years.

Our efforts paid off, and it was very gratifying. Fourteen firms said "yes." The fifteenth firm decided to go another route, but changed their minds a few years later and joined us. As other large firms saw what we were doing, they became interested in becoming members.

LEA'S FOUR CORE PRINCIPLES

We were a very entrepreneurial group. By August 1999, all the pieces were in place and we were ready to draft our core principles. We had four, and they all were pretty straightforward:

There was no limit on firms competing against each other in the same market. We reasoned that you can't stop great firms from growing into different markets. The current M&A climate in the accounting industry bears this out. Firms are acquiring other firms in cities that already are represented in their associations. The Internet, which was pretty much in its nascence when LEA was formed, leveled the playing field. Physical location isn't the barrier to doing business that it once was.

Culture happens from the top down, and best practices are a big part of culture. Nothing big happens at a firm without the managing partner's involvement; no new programs are implemented and no investments in technology are made. That's why we made managing partner involvement a part of the firm's commitment to LEA. As the saying goes, "You don't know what you don't know." We believed that involving a group of managing partners that didn't believe the status quo was always the best way forward would open the door to bigger and better things for all member firms.

LEA was designed as a best practices exchange for the firm-as-a-whole. Managing partner participation was the key, but we wanted the free exchange of new ideas and best practices at different levels across the firm. We wanted a 360-degree view, so we organized special interest groups (or SIGs) that spanned the entire firm from firm operations to services and industries. Our SIGs included managing partners, rising stars, marketing and business development, human resources and firm administration, and numerous service and industry niches such as tax, SALT, restaurants, nonprofits and manufacturing. In the end, we probably created well over 100 SIGs.

Relationships are important in business. We wanted our association to encourage relationships that encouraged trust and became friendships. To accomplish this, we designed LEA to treat its member firms as clients. To facilitate relationship building between firm counterparts, and especially across each SIG, we scheduled regular SIG meetings throughout the year. Groups meet regularly to discuss challenges and best practices. Some meetings are in-person and others are virtual. The strategy worked. Many of our members have formed true friendships that have endured across mergers and miles.

Through the years we continued to add member firms. Sometimes firms approached us, sometimes we actively recruited firms that met our idea of progressive firms that were interested in growing and adapting to changes in areas like technology, firm operations, database management, marketing and business development. These firms spanned the U.S. and ranged in size from relatively small to large. Size and location were very definitely not among the criteria we measured.

RECRUITING INTERNATIONAL FIRMS

LEA's international arm developed in a similar way. At first, we affiliated with an international association comprised of smaller firms. When it turned out these firms couldn't handle the sophisticated work we wanted to send them, we decided to form our own association of like-minded international firms.

I invited about 10 firms to a meeting in London. I knew some of these firms from the other associations we'd been in. We mirrored the process we'd used in the U.S. but, because of our success there, the process was quicker. Firms in other parts of the world noticed us and asked to join.

SUCCESS

By 2015, LEA was the second largest alliance of CPA firms in the world with total revenues approaching $3 billion dollars and a well-respected international board. LEA's 220 member firms operate in 106 countries, giving clients of LEA Global firms access to 2,000 experts and nearly 23,000 staff members. Of LEA's 50 plus member firms in the U.S., 40 are listed among the nation's top 200 firms.

A BITTERSWEET MOMENT

On a bittersweet note, when SS&G was acquired by BDO in January 2015, it joined a firm with its own a $7 billion international association. And you know what that meant: the moment we became part of BDO we ceased to be part of LEA. It was very difficult for me.

It was a tremendous amount of fun building LEA. I did have a chance in January 2015 to go to the LEA meeting and say my good-byes, and tell them a little bit about what happened and explain why our firm made the decision.

Even though that chapter's over, the friendships are still in place. I'll be grateful for that for the rest of my life.

winning
is everything

Chapter 4

WINNING IS EVERYTHING

ACKNOWLEDGEMENTS

The Advisory Board members are some of the most impressive consultants I have ever met—Jay Nisberg, Troy Waugh, Rebecca Ryan, Gary Boomer, and Allan Koltin. And we were supported by Kathy Sautters and Jeannette Schwartz-Ruttan.

A special shout out to Allan Koltin. "My brother from another mother." A dear friend and colleague.

* * * * *

Great practice management has a ripple effect: a positive culture helps the firm attract and retain talented professionals and keeps everyone invested in the firm's success. All managing partners are interested in best practices in their areas of responsibility, including modeling the firm's culture, which begins with him or her, and overseeing the operational and technical aspects of running the firm. Some of these things are practical while others are intangible.

That is one reason practice management conferences have been part of the accounting firm landscape since at least the 1980s. Managing partners want to understand what other firms, especially best-of-the-best firms, are doing.

Prior to 1999, there were several practice management conferences whose primary focus was best practices for running a firm. One was sponsored by a group of publishers and consultants, another by the AICPA, and still others by state societies that held Managing Accounting Practice (MAP) conferences. For one reason or another, these conferences fell out of favor and no one was providing a venue for best practices in practice management.

Then, in 1999, Jay Nisberg coordinated a meeting between myself, him, Allan Koltin and Gary Boomer. I'd worked with Jay at various times, and I knew Allan and Gary from the conferences I attended. The goal was starting a conference that would fill the gap.

The three of us met at the Hilton O'Hare for an entire day. At the end of that day, we decided to form a business entity called The Advisory Board and use it to resurrect the idea of a practice management conference.

We moved quickly. We planned our first conference for later in the year, immediately after the AICPA's Major Firms Conference in Naples, Florida. We thought planning it that way was a smart idea. After all, a lot managing partners would already be in Naples. Why wouldn't they stay for our conference?

Well, they didn't. We had about 60 attendees, and most of those were sponsors. To add insult to injury, our conference was held at the Ritz-Carlton at Tiburon. Great venue, but not the day of our conference—which was the same day as the hotel's grand opening. They were totally disorganized and unprepared. It was a disaster, but it was also an eye-opening experience.

LEARNING FROM FAILURE; BUILDING ON SUCCESS

The first conference was far from the success we'd envisioned. Nevertheless, some elements resonated with the attendees, particularly the agenda which we had carefully planned. We all felt we were on to something that could succeed. We decided to try it again, but tweak it to incorporate the parts our attendees liked.

Outside Voices. Planning is always my starting point. So, as always, research was the initial step in planning for the first conference. Part of that research included reviewing the agendas for other conferences. Most of them featured accountants speaking to other accountants.

The four of us understood the value in that, but we also recognized that other professions and industries are run by pretty smart people who have ideas we'd never thought about. I'd seen that first hand when I started SS&G's restaurant niche. It was going to a restaurant industry conference that made me realize how easy it is for people in an industry, any industry, to become insular. Many in accounting, for example, look at what their competitor firms are doing and try to mimic their successes.

But every firm is different—its culture, its talents, its goals. What works for Firm A might not work for Firm B. That's why it's so important to look outside of your world and at least be aware of what others are doing. Hearing speakers from other industries was one of the things that resonated with the attendees at our first conference. We built on this, and over the years we've brought in interesting speakers from throughout the business and sports worlds. We brought in visionaries; founders of innovative companies like Southwest Airlines and Adidas; sports figures who shared thoughts on teamwork and things of that nature. We always look for interesting people who can educate us. We've had some amazing speakers who have given us awesome insights.

Networking. The other thing we did right from the start was to build in a lot of networking time so managing partners could start building relationships and exchange ideas with others at the conference.

Most of us come back from meetings, especially practice management meetings, with ideas we want to implement. Even if we don't want to admit it, being a managing partner can be isolating in some ways. Being in a room with peers you like and trust is a catalyst for the free exchange of ideas and best practices. It took us a few years to build this component of the conference, but I believe it is one of the most valuable aspects of the conference, which we called "Winning Is Everything."

Venue. We also decided to move the venue to Las Vegas. We chose Vegas for two reasons: it's fairly easy to get to from anywhere in the country, and accountants liked going there. That turned out to be a good decision, and a lasting one. The conference has been held in Vegas ever since.

The second year was much more successful than the first. We had 100 attendees, and most of our sponsors came back even though they had an awful experience in year one. We grew again in year three, and in succeeding years. We created a large community of followers, and eventually, we had hundreds of CPAs at the event.

Overcoming our dismal performance in year one was challenging; it's not easy to overcome a negative first impression. But we believed in our concept and worked hard to make Winning Is Everything one of the industry's premier events.

The Great Recession of 2008 affected our attendance, and it took us a few years to get the numbers back up. Today, however, Winning Is Everything is the largest and most well-attended conference of managing partners of major CPA firms in the world. It attracts people from Australia, Europe, Asia, Mexico, South America as well as from throughout the United States.

THINK TWICE BEFORE FOREGOING AN INFRASTRUCTURE

Unlike most of the businesses I've been involved with, we didn't initially have an infrastructure for Winning Is Everything. We really struggled with the ramifications in the early days, and I'm not sure I would do it the same way again.

We didn't do this blindly. There were numerous reasons we took this route, but the main one was that we weren't sure whether an annual conference like ours would have legs. We didn't want to hire a staff for what might be a one-time project, so we began without a dedicated person to run our conference. That meant no one to keep a database of attendees, sponsors, or payments. There was no one to oversee the actual event planning either; and no one person had responsibility for developing relationships at the hotel or overseeing the space requirements or catering. Our experience at the Ritz-Carlton in Tiburon taught us, as if we didn't know, that we don't know everything and we aren't good at everything. So even though we saw the conference grow, it was very disorganized.

Chaos isn't a space where I operate well. Once we were convinced we were going to keep the conference going we were ready to hire an Executive Director.

At the three-year mark, we offered the position to Kathy Sautters. Kathy was SS&G's marketing person. She was leaving that position to move to Connecticut. We all agreed Kathy was the right person to help run The Advisory Board and Winning Is Everything. It was January 2001, the very beginning of telecommuting. Working remotely, Kathy stayed on as Executive Director for about 12 years. She ended up leaving us to continue her career elsewhere in the accounting profession.

We tried going in a new direction with our next conference director, but that didn't work out. Finally, about three years ago, we ended up asking my assistant, Jeannette Schwartz-Ruttan, if she would consider taking over the conference.

Jeannette had never been involved in Winning Is Everything and needed to learn everything from the bottom up. She was a quick study, though, and things are again running smoothly on the operational end.

SPONSORSHIPS

One of the ways the conference makes money is through sponsorships. Many large companies offering goods and services to the accounting industry have sponsored Winning Is Everything. It is a win-win: they pay us a fee and in return they gain exposure to managing partners and other C-level executives of some of the largest firms in the United States as well as internationally.

Sponsorships are another whole aspect of conferences. Tiered levels of sponsorships need to be part of the deal: software providers and publishers; recruiters; consultants who offer various services, from M&A to training; membership associations and state societies. There are many variables, from discounts for multi-attendees to levels of exposure to attendees. All are part of conference operations. Having a dedicated—and detail-oriented—operations person who is able to nurture relationships is critical to any successful business, and Winning Is Everything is no exception.

CONSTANTLY TWEAK THE KNOWLEDGE BASE

While some topics are evergreen and should be updated annually, like the state of the industry and new technology, that is not enough to make a conference successful. Other topics must be included, and those need to change and flow along with what is happening in the industry: Succession planning. Merger and acquisition. Marketing and business development. Generational shifts. Culture and diversity. Globalization. Blockchain. AI. These reflect issues that are shaping the firms of the future and the industry in general. They are the meat of what future-forward attendees want to learn about and understand.

Through the years, we've reflected these developments at Winning Is Everything. From talking about the issues that personally affect members of The Advisory Board to looking outside of accounting, to featuring how marketing and business development have impacted the way firms operate, we've covered many of the threats and opportunities the industry faces.

Another thing we've done is to keep attracting new attendees. Over time, we've tried to do this by including additional syllabi specifically targeted to specific audiences: human resources professionals, women and rising stars. Currently, we have a specific marketing and business development track. While some firms still don't understand the importance of branding and selling, progressive firms view those functions as integral to their success. The professionals that attend Winning Is Everything are considered part of the C-suite, just as in any other business. We've also begun a webinar series.

Our efforts are a good example of how businesses evolve, but Winning Is Everything remains the foundation for it all.

KEEP TWEAKING

Winning Is Everything was designed as a vehicle for exposing our target audience—accountants and business advisors—to best practices from outside of our industry. We've done that ever since our first conference, and the audience loves it. But we had another objective too: We wanted our attendees to find the conference a safe place for the free exchange of ideas. A place where managing partners can talk about what does and doesn't work for them. Our managing partner sessions have yielded some great ideas that enabled firms to nurture great firm cultures.

We always ask our managing partners about their goals. Personally, it is validating that none of the managing partners at our conferences has ever listed "profitability" as a goal. Chasing dollars for their own sake, without a supporting strategy, is not a recipe for long-term success. Recognizing opportunities when they arise and being able to adjust to include them in your strategic plan in a synergistic way is what feeds a thriving business. What works for one doesn't work for all, but some version of it might.

At this point, we want to continue to grow Winning Is Everything. We understand the industry's "extreme M&A" environment, but we believe there always will be room for entrepreneurial firms that want to test the limits of the norm. That's why we continue to incorporate relevant add-ons that will help boost attendees' efforts to keep their firms relevant.

Chapter 5

HILLEL AT KENT STATE UNIVERSITY

ACKNOWLEDGEMENTS

Hillel at Kent State was a true partnership with Jennifer Chestnut. Our partnership was supported by Joe Kanfer, Gary Cohn, Vic and Ellen Cohn and a terrific board.

* * * * *

THE BACK STORY: FULFILLING A 30-YEAR-OLD VISION

The Hillel chapter at Kent State University started in the 1970s. Building a permanent home for it was a 30-year-old Jewish Federation of Cleveland dream that never happened—until the day in 2004 I met with Bill Heller, a long-time friend and fellow CPA, and the project was reborn.

When Bill asked to meet with me, I had no idea what he had in mind. At the time, the Jewish Federation of Cleveland was celebrating its centennial and the theme was Growing Jewish Cleveland. Kent State is located about 40 miles or so from Cleveland, not quite local but close enough to be attractive to young college students. The Foundation for Jewish Campus Life (simply known as Hillel International or Hillel), is the largest Jewish campus organization in the world, working with thousands of college students across the globe. There are about 550 chapters worldwide.

At our meeting, Bill asked me to become president of the board and lead the building effort. I was completely blindsided. Why had they come to me? I was involved with Federation, but was not involved with Hillel. I was flattered, but naturally had some reservations.

Earlier in my career, I probably would have dived right in without truly grasping the nuances. By 2004, though, I was savvy enough to understand what a project like this entailed. Before deciding whether I wanted to be involved, I decided to take a step back and really think about what my involvement would require.

I went through a careful thought process, understanding what I needed in place to be successful: a capital campaign chair; a committed board; continuing dialogue with the university and the university president.

The Jewish Federation of Cleveland was ready to invest in the project, which was a good thing. The rest had to be put in place before we could even talk about the new building. So, what would it take to make me say "yes"?

The three pillars of my decision were:

- Belief this was giving back to the community

- Willingness to spend the time needed—which is always a multiple of however long you think it will be

- Understanding what needs to happen to make it work, from getting funding to understanding the demographics of the target audience to hiring architects, contractors, and the like. These factors are the cornerstones of a workable strategic plan.

Each of those boxes got checked off. I was in.

Becoming involved with building the Hillel at Kent State opened another chapter of my life. Today, I'm one of about 20 members on Hillel's international board.

WHERE IS KENT STATE AGAIN?

My due diligence included a trip to Kent State. Initially, and embarrassingly, I didn't even know where in my state it was located. (It's about 12 miles from Akron.)

I went and, over dinner, Bill and I met with a few board members and Jennifer Chestnut, who was then-Executive Director of Kent State Hillel.

One of the things I learned was that Gordon Gee, then-President of The Ohio State University, was supportive of having Hillels on his campus. He'd also supported them at Brown and Vanderbilt, where he had previously served as president. Other college presidents noticed and encouraged them as well. In places like Syracuse, Indiana and Michigan, the anecdotal evidence showed a correlation between having a Hillel on campus and attracting Jewish students.

As a result, Dr. Carol Cartwright, then-university president, was fully behind our endeavor. She agreed the Hillel building should be on the campus, and identified a piece of land for it. I was impressed, and came away determined to chair the project.

THE BIG PICTURE VIEW COMES FIRST

Where to start? At the very beginning of a project like this, you need to be able to float above it, take a mental snapshot of what it will take to get to the finish line, and then map a route. If you get mired in the details too early on, it becomes too difficult to move ahead. This is something I learned through the years. You need to have a big picture view before you get down to the nitty gritty. If you do it the other way, it becomes impossible to see your goal.

Some "first tier" issues we needed to consider included:

- Could we get the capital we needed to fund a building that ultimately cost more than $4 million?

- What hurdles would we have to clear to get the land we needed?

- Did we have the leadership talent to spearhead the project?

- Were there any tricky issues that had to be navigated? (In this case, the biggest challenge was replacing an inactive board with one that was ready to make things happen.)

Our analysis told us we had a viable project. We then moved on to the next level of priorities, which were more nuts-and-bolts:

- How would we figure out what functions we needed the building to fulfill?

- How big should the building be?

- How would we decide on an architect and a construction company?

Parsing the thought process for getting a project—or a business—off the ground is the same. The degree of difficulty in each successive level of issues doesn't necessarily change. The important thing is drilling down and making sure there is a clear path for getting things done in a way that makes sense and moves the project forward.

When dealing with a nonprofit, personnel issues can be problematic. You're dealing with volunteers, everyone wants a say, and everyone knows "the best" person to provide a service. Navigating the personalities of board members and major contributors is one of the most important aspects of leading a project like this one. You must be prepared to have difficult conversations.

BUILDING A STRATEGY

Jen Chestnut and I, who were the group's leaders, sat down to hash out exactly how to proceed. There are issues that arise in building a nonprofit that don't come up in other types of businesses. We came up with a list of five critical items:

1. **The Board of Directors**: Most of the existing board came from outside of the Cleveland area, but we wanted to make it more of a regional entity. We also had to decide how many people we wanted on the board; who we wanted to serve on it; who we wanted to resign; and who should chair the board.

2. **Board structure:** What committees would we need and how would the chairperson of each be determined?

3. **Outsourcing:** What would our process be for deciding on critical hires—architect, contractors, interior designer, etc.? This can be very tricky when you are dealing with suggestions made by volunteers, especially high-profile donors.

4. **Fundraising:** How would we identify potential big donors and donors in general? Who would lead our capital campaign?

5. **Sustainability over the long term:** How would we make this Hillel sustainable over the long term?

This list is not definitive, but it is apparent that some of the items are political. How could we navigate this delicately and without alienating anybody? Building in processes averted some potential problems. Jen was vital to the rest. She had the right political instincts and diplomatic skills to minimize the fallout from difficult conversations. We knew we were lucky to have someone on our team who had the right leadership skills. Having the right people in place is critical to the success of any business venture.

OVERARCHING CHALLENGES

Raising money is always a challenge. In the case of our Hillel, the challenge was bigger than I ever imagined. That was because we started our project while the Jewish Federation of Cleveland's Centennial Campaign was going on. The Federation promised us $2 million in funding, which was wonderful, but in exchange we had to agree not to solicit the people on their list.

This was a huge barrier, especially when you realize that 85 percent of Kent State graduates come from the Cleveland area, and only a small percentage of them are Jewish. That meant our raw list of about 200,000 alumni names boiled down to about 10,000 potential donors, and we could only appeal to about 1,500 of them. (Ohio's Jewish population is roughly 1.3 percent of the state's total population)

Another big challenge was getting the Ohio General Assembly to enact Ohio Board of Regents' Rule 3333-1-03, which appropriated $400,000 in capital funds for the building under the terms of a Joint Use Agreement. In December 2007, after many rounds of negotiation, the bill was passed.

FUNDRAISING 101

Hillel at Kent State was built before LinkedIn, Kickstarter, Facebook, Twitter or Snapchat. There were no Google searches. It's amazing to think that was only about 11 years ago. So, we had to use printouts of lists and manually go through them. We literally sat around a table looking for the names of potential donors and figuring out who knows who. It was a labor-intensive process.

Our starting point was the state's geography. Kent State is located close to Youngstown, Akron and Canton, but much of the school's population comes from the Cleveland area. Most of the board came from Cleveland as well. Our goal of making the board more of a regional entity was accomplished when Joe Kanfer, president of Akron-based Gojo Industries, Inc., the inventor of Purell, agreed to lead the capital campaign.

At first, we tried to cull the Kent State alumni list for donors ourselves. But it was so time-consuming we knew we had to find another way.

We sent the list to what was essentially a big data firm and asked them to determine who might be Jewish. The result was a list with 10,000 names—much better. We then vetted that list to eliminate those who might be on the Federation's donor list. That left us with approximately 1,500 names, 100 of whom had the potential to give big donations. Jennifer oversaw the campaign for most of the list. Her efforts involved mostly snail mail and email requests for donations. The response was good—but it takes a lot of $5, $10 and $20 gifts to add up to the amount of money we needed.

Joe, Jen and I took responsibility for seeking donations from the 100-name short list. Over the course of about two years, we met with everyone on the list. We faced a lot of rejection, but we didn't let that stop us. It was just part of the process, as it always is when you start a business.

MAKING MAGIC HAPPEN

It didn't happen overnight, but word of the project got out in the community. Eventually, in 2010, Joe and I wound up meeting with Victor Cohn, a former president of the Hillel board and a prominent local businessman. At the meeting, I asked Victor if I could solicit his son Gary, then President of Goldman Sachs, for a donation. Gary recently served as Director of President Donald J. Trump's National Economic Council.

Victor said he'd rather we didn't, but didn't say we couldn't. (It really is better to ask forgiveness rather than permission.)

Joe and I decided to go ahead and try. We brainstormed, and decided it was best to indirectly approach Gary. We agreed meeting Gary at an upcoming Jewish Federation event in New York City, where he lived, was the best option.

Remember, this was pre-social media. So, while getting an introduction might be easier today, we probably still would have opted for an in-person meeting. There is something about a face-to-face meeting that can't be replicated. That's as true today as it ever was. You can't look into someone's eyes, read their body language, or develop instant rapport on a social media,

VoIP or video conferencing platform. For sure, these tools are invaluable to all kinds of businesses, but there is something unique about face-to-face interactions. Sometimes, as in this instance, it's the best way to proceed even though travel costs and other incidentals are incurred.

It was kind of funny. We were worried about the New York Federation's connection with Gary, but we were cleared to speak with him.

It was arranged that Joe would sit at Gary's table at the New York City event. The rest was up to him.

The two of them had a conversation that opened the door to further discussion. And, after several further meetings, Gary told us he would make a major donation if we agreed to name the building in honor of his parents, Victor and Ellen Cohn.

In explaining why he chose to make this gift to Hillel at Kent State, Gary said, "In making this gift, I was thinking about three things: How to celebrate the milestone birthdays of both my mother and my father, who were turning 75; how I could give back to Northeast Ohio where I have my roots; and what organization would be meaningful to my family both now and in the future."

There, in a nutshell, is an example of the passion and dedication needed for success. Gary's goals were very personal, but that only added to his desire to be a part of the project.

This is how it is if you are someone who is driven to succeed. Once you commit to doing something—whether that thing is big or small—you are all in. Whatever it takes to get it done.

In the case of Kent State Hillel, Gary Cohn's gift put us over the fundraising finish line. His gift also allowed us to seed an endowment fund that would maintain the Hillel for many years. And now, we were ready to build the Cohn Jewish Student Center.

PATIENCE AND PERSEVERANCE

It took five years from the time I became involved in the project to the grand opening of the 14,000-square foot Cohn Jewish Student Center. Along the way, we overcame bureaucratic red tape, personality issues, and lack of sufficient funding. We succeeded because we looked at each of these hurdles as challenges rather than roadblocks. If one tactic failed, we looked for another way to succeed.

Yes, we got discouraged at times, but we never let it stop us. We learned, kept going and kept growing. Commitment matters. Things usually take longer and cost more than you initially think.

Successful negotiations always are give and take. There were some non-negotiables, of course, but the process was a fascinating learning experience. I'm not a particularly patient person, but I discovered that there is no way to get around certain things. Working with the state bureaucracy to get something done takes persistence, not personality. We couldn't get around it, so we simply plowed through.

We had a lot of donors, small and big, and each of them truly believed in what we were doing. The idea for a Hillel at Kent State had been on the horizon for decades. It took a few people who were able and willing to develop and follow a strategic plan, be flexible and creative about workarounds when it came to challenges and use their connections. The vision become reality.

Today, the Cohn Jewish Student Center is a vital part of campus life at Kent State. It has small and large conference rooms, a chapel, a lounge and a banquet/party room. The only Jewish institution in Portage County, the Center has hosted its share of weddings and funerals over the years.

GROWING MONEY

One of the underpinnings of our plan was figuring out how to create an endowment that would allow the Kent State Hillel to be self-sustaining and remain viable over time. This became somewhat easier because Gary's gift put us $2 million over our $4 million target, but we still needed a plan.

We wound up with a complicated financing arrangement under which we issued bonds guaranteed by the Jewish Federation of Cleveland. I took the corpus of our principal and created an arbitrage. Instead of using the $4 million cash we'd raised to pay for the building, we took out a mortgage at a favorable rate. We took the cash and invested it in the Jewish Federation of Cleveland at a higher rate than we paid on the mortgage. The difference between what we paid and what we earned created significant cash flow for Hillel.

The Cohn Jewish Student Center at Kent State University

The energy of Engage!

Chapter 6

BUILDING
ENGAGE! CLEVELAND

ACKNOWLEDGEMENTS

Engage! Cleveland didn't happen without the knowledge sharing and encouragement of Rebecca Ryan. Or without the skills of Ashley Basile-Oeken, Andrew Bennett, Mariann Crosley, Evan Ishida, Lauren Rudman, and Kim Pesses. Thank you all.

And a special thanks to Ira Kaplan for taking the lead.

* * * * *

MAKING CLEVELAND A DESTINATION
FOR YOUNG PEOPLE

In the early 2000s, I was introduced to Rebecca Ryan. She was a consultant who had been engaged by the City of Akron to develop a strategy to attract young professionals. Rebecca's work was funded through a contribution made by First Energy to work with the City of Akron. Over dinner, she told me a bit about her company, Next Generation Consulting, which teaches municipalities and large corporations how to be the employer of choice and the location of choice for the next generation.

I was fascinated because I was seeing the other end of this in my personal life and my business. Neither of my two then-college-aged kids were planning to return to the Cleveland area after graduation. At my CPA firm, it was very difficult to attract high level talent. We needed a certain number of young professionals to make our engine run, but Northeast Ohio had no caché. It wasn't a desirable place to live and work.

As Rebecca and I talked, I had an epiphany. I learned that two important shifts had happened while I wasn't watching:

- When I graduated college, big cities like Chicago and New York were desirable destinations. Today's young professionals can choose to work in any big city anywhere in the world: Paris or Brussels, Taiwan or South Africa. The whole dynamic had flipped, and it made the competition for talent much fiercer.

- Today, three out of four young professionals pick where they want to live *before* they have a job. This is completely contrary to my generation's approach: for us, the job had to be there first.

After that dinner, I found myself preoccupied with our conversation. I was born and raised in Cleveland. I love the city. I kept thinking "Why isn't Cleveland hiring Rebecca? We have so many attractive resources— professional sports, colleges and universities, restaurants, low cost of living, one of the five best art museums in the world, a world-class orchestra. We have everything. Why aren't young people coming here?"

I learned that cities throughout the Midwest and elsewhere were looking at Rebecca and others like her to help develop strategies to attract and retain young professionals.

My belief in the concept deepened: there's nothing more valuable to a city like Cleveland than attracting young people to seed and grow it going forward, long term. It's always about a sustainable future, whether you are talking about a business or a city.

Of the cities that had begun similar initiatives, Denver, Nashville, Philadelphia and Milwaukee were of interest. Each of them was attempting to attract young professionals by rebuilding their city centers and reconfiguring them with restaurants and other venues designed to draw a hip, young crowd. Each was also trying to persuade companies of all sizes and cultures to move there and bring with them good jobs at companies of all sizes.

Closer to home, Akron, Columbus and Cincinnati had all started programs. I thought it would be easy to start a Cleveland initiative. I would get the city to own it and the Chamber of Commerce to get involved and Cleveland would be on the bandwagon. But I was wrong. It wasn't easy at all. Over about five years, I must have had a hundred meetings with County Commissioners, the Mayor, the Governor, the Chancellor of Ohio universities, state representatives—and anyone else I thought could help me launch this project. It was incredibly difficult to generate buy-in.

THERE ARE NO DEAD ENDS

When working with nonprofits, there are two elements that make the effort successful: somebody must own it and somebody must fund it. I couldn't get either, and became very discouraged.

Then in 2010, Jennifer Thomas, who worked for Fund for Economic Future in Cleveland, made a suggestion that really turned everything around: "Maybe you should consider starting from the bottom up and instead of the top down."

Whoa!

My experience in business had taught me that, with connections, I could more easily get things done if I started high and moved down. But that wasn't working in this situation and I needed to try something different.

By definition, entrepreneurs are open to new ideas. My belief that revitalizing Cleveland would attract young professionals hadn't changed, but I'd learned that the traditional "it's who you know" theory of growing a business wasn't working. If I continued doing the same things repeatedly, I'd only become more frustrated. So, I ran with Jennifer's suggestion to start at the bottom.

Initially, I raised $12,500—including $2,500 of my own money—and organized a young professionals summit. I hired Rebecca to come in and speak. We ended up having 300 people at the summit, including young professionals, seasoned professionals and politicians.

We spent the morning talking about what had to happen to make Cleveland attractive to young professionals. We had an audience, which was wonderful, but we still didn't have a champion.

Then, a woman in the audience said some things that helped turn things around. Her name was Cindy Schulz, and she was the Chief Communication Officer for The Cleveland Foundation, which is a premier community foundation.

I spoke with her after the meeting and learned Cindy was really interested in this idea because, like me, she had college-age kids who didn't plan on returning to Cleveland. I followed up with her, and she ended up making introductions to some of the grant makers at The Cleveland Foundation. I assembled a PowerPoint presentation outlining why they should help fund this initiative and get it off the ground.

The Cleveland Foundation thought the idea had value. They wanted to talk to me again after I partnered with someone who was more process-oriented than I was. They suggested I work with Marianne Crosley, head of the Cleveland Leadership Center.

Marianne essentially became my partner, adding the practical skills needed to balance to my entrepreneurial talents. We wound up being paired with a group, YPConnect, a collaboration of 60-65 different YP organizations all over the city. YPConnect's member groups were quite granular: each served a particular cultural or professional community. Some overlapped. So, for example, someone who was in the Cleveland accountants group might or might not also be a member of the Hispanic Clevelanders group. Essentially, our goal was to become the umbrella organization for all the groups.

YPConnect became the basis for launching Engage! Cleveland. Once we came together and facilitated the beginning of Engage! Cleveland, the Cleveland Foundation funded us with a little under $200,000.

One of the first things we did was create a working board, which turned into a formal board. We got help from many businesses, including Paul Clark, the president of PNC, and Barry Doggett, a senior vice president at Eaton Corp. A few of the larger organizations involved agreed to contribute.

Engage! Cleveland launched in 2012. I love the name Engage! Cleveland because it so clearly describes our goal of engaging, attracting and retaining young professionals. At launch, Ashley Basile-Oeken, who we hired as Executive Director, was our only employee.

DEVISING A STRATEGY

As we planned our strategy, we looked closely at what other communities both inside and outside Ohio were doing. We didn't want to reinvent the wheel but we also wanted something that was tailored to our city and its unique idiosyncrasies. That was our research piece. Once that was done, we honed our plan to be specifically tailor-made for Cleveland.

At the urging of The Cleveland Foundation, we partnered with a group called Global Cleveland. Global Cleveland's mission—attracting people to Cleveland—was similar to ours. The difference was the target audience. We were appealing to young professionals; they were targeting immigrants. After about six months, it was obvious the organizations were going in different directions. We negotiated an exit from Global Cleveland and moved to the Greater Cleveland Partnership, which was essentially the Chamber of Commerce. They incubated us. We worked out of their offices, and they provided some support.

During that time, we were trying to figure out our next steps. Although we had set a strategy, it became clear some of our tactics were not working. Giving up wasn't an option, so we sat down again and brainstormed new ideas for making our mandate come to life.

TRIAL AND ERROR

We tried several different approaches. Again, some things worked and others didn't.

This venture was unlike anything I'd been involved with before. The board, which was a big issue in Hillel, wasn't a problem here. Instead, the challenge was ephemeral: we were trying to attract an audience that had no idea they needed our services. So, we kept trying different things until we started seeing some success. Three stand out:

- Our quarterly mixer events turned out to be one of our most popular ventures. The mixers were held in cultural and other venues throughout the city. We held them at the Art Museum, the Natural History Museum and the Cleveland Botanical Gardens. Thousands of young professionals came, many of whom had never been to these venues. They began engaging the community, just as we'd hoped.

- Helping colleges, universities and corporations sell the community was another priority. We found that orientation tours for university students and company employees was effective because it showcased the city's many attractions.

- The Engage! Cleveland website was another important project. We spent a lot of time on the design of the site and the message. We wanted it to stand as a good selling tool for Cleveland.

I'm not sure why these tactics worked when others failed, but that isn't the point. The important thing is that we didn't give up. We viewed our failures as learning opportunities. We massaged what was working; tweaked marginal efforts to be better; jettisoned efforts that weren't working; and tried new approaches.

We kept pushing ahead, brainstorming, getting new funding—we pursued all avenues so our entrepreneurial endeavor could succeed. We continue to explore new ways to reach young professionals so that they keep responding to our message.

In a way, this is the most creative project I've ever been involved in. Our mission was to involve everyone in our target demographic—it didn't matter what career they were pursuing and we had few restrictions on the methods we could use to attract them.

ATTRACTING BUSINESSES TO NORTHEAST OHIO

Ask me and I'll tell you what a great place Cleveland is for raising a family. Ask non-Clevelanders what they think and the answers are far different. From our weather, which really isn't that different than big Northeast cities like New York and Boston, to being a city in disrepair, their general impression is negative.

Changing people's opinion of Cleveland was, and is, a major goal for Engage! Cleveland. People aren't interested in living and working in a place that doesn't appeal to their sensibilities. How do you begin to change a negative perception to a positive one? The city was undergoing a revitalization, and we rode the tailwinds. Office buildings were being converted into apartments; several entertainment districts, Playhouse Square and the casino were undergoing renovation; the Republican National Convention came to town; the Cleveland Indians and the Cleveland Cavaliers had good seasons. Downtown Cleveland was transformed and an entirely new stock of housing upped the ante.

The focus on jobs resulted in huge rewards. Quicken Loans invested in Engage! Cleveland, JumpStart, Inc. committed to helping Cleveland's entrepreneurs succeed, and the accomplishments of organizations like the world-renowned Cleveland Clinic created many jobs. It's a slow process, but our efforts showed measurable progress and we've ranked well on lists of cities with brain gain.

YPCLEVELAND WEEK: THE GAME CHANGER

In 2014, we held our first YPCleveland event. It was similar to one held in Milwaukee, but we adapted it for the features that make Cleveland unique.

The week-long agenda we developed was comprised of morning, afternoon, and evening events all over the city. The events were organized strategically: morning events often had a physical component like spin classes or yoga classes in different parts of the city; afternoon sessions usually were held downtown with a relevant speaker at a cool venue like the baseball stadium; evening events were similar with speakers or panels discussing topics relevant to young professionals.

Thousands of people participated. We got great press and word-of-mouth.

All of this made us made us rethink our business model. Our goal was to become a self-sustaining entity that didn't have to rely on grants to keep us going. So, in 2015, we kept similar programming but charged modest fees to attend. Attendance remained the same, and we raised enough money to cover the costs and fund the organization for one year. It was exciting, and it showed us we were really onto something important to the future of our city. We believed we had enough community interest to be viable over the long term.

ON OUR OWN

We made some major decisions that allowed us to become even more self-sufficient. Led by Ira Kaplan, Engage! Cleveland's board chair, we left the Greater Cleveland Partnership and became a nonprofit in our own name.

For 2016, we tried a tiered membership model. Annual membership fees ranged from $50 for individual members to $250 for young professional organizations to $5,000 for employers with over 1,000 employees. Each successive tier came with its own set of benefits. Our 2017 event had over 2,400 attendees, 94 percent of whom were between the ages of 22 and 35 years old.

BELIEVE IN THE PROJECT; BELIEVE IN YOURSELF; BELIEVE THE PATH TO SUCCESS IS ROCKY

All of this grew from a dinner with Rebecca Ryan back in 2005. It was a lot of work, and for much of that time there was little reward. But I truly believed attracting, retaining and engaging young professionals was vital to Cleveland's future, and I was willing to support the efforts any way I could—including putting my money where my mouth was.

Every baby step forward was a step closer to realizing something I passionately believed in. Today, Engage! Cleveland is an important element of the city's development plan. It has become an accepted vehicle for bringing together the young professionals and businesses that are so important to the Cleveland's future.

Residents of NCCH

Chapter 7

NORTH COAST COMMUNITY HOMES (NCCH)

ACKNOWLEDGEMENTS

Steve McPeake, thank you for taking me on this special journey that impacted so many challenged people in our community. I learned so much from you and this experience.

* * * * *

Since childhood, I've been concerned with and passionate about the care of disables individuals. It was and is a very personal interest.

My late brother, David, had a non-cancerous brain tumor removed when he was two years old. The surgery resulted in severe mental disabilities. When he was five, my parents decided it was best to move him into a facility that could properly care for him. I was only eight years old at the time, but I remember they considered state facilities and psychiatric institutions for patients with mental retardation and other developmental handicaps. Even then, these types of facilities generally operated under a cloud of perceived abuse and misconduct.

My parents struggled with the idea of David living in a place like that, so they went in a different direction. They moved him into a private home in Milan, Ohio, which cared for people with similar struggles. Every third Sunday until he passed away at the age of 18, my family would pile into the car to make the two-hour ride to Milan and spend the day with David.

Looking back, I was so proud of the decision my parents made regarding my brother. He lived in a warm and caring environment, with dignity and love.

It was tough, and I learned a lot about life at a very early age. As I matured into a teenager and young adult, my impressions molded into deep compassion for the residents of that home—individuals who faced incredible challenges. In many ways, I am grateful to have seen what it was like for people who were so afflicted through no fault of their own. I think it made me a better and more caring person. But there was a big price to pay.

After I moved back to Cleveland, I joined the Citizens Advisory Board for the Broadview Developmental Campus. Broadview Development was a state of Ohio facility that supposedly cared for individuals with mental disabilities. The Citizens Advisory Board was in place to serve as a liaison among—and watchdog for—the community, state of Ohio, and the residents.

The fact that my brother could have wound up in such a facility was incredibly disturbing. The living conditions were intolerable. The residents were abused in ways I don't feel comfortable disclosing. The local newspapers had articles almost daily about the conditions of the campus, as well as the behavior of the employees. It was a disgrace. There was no dignity. There was no caring. There was only abuse.

In the 1970s, then-Governor of Ohio, John Gilligan, brought changes to the system that had been successfully implemented in other states on the east coast. Among them was an initiative to empty the existing campuses and establish a new stock of housing for the residents in local communities via small group homes. It took several years for the ideas to gain traction, but about a decade later, in the mid-1980s, the idea for North Coast Community Homes was born.

I was introduced to NCCH's founder, Stephen McPeake, in 1983, about a year before he founded the organization. Steve had received start-up funding from The Cleveland Foundation, and my firm was hired as his fledgling organization's first accounting firm.

At the time, I did not have a board position at NCCH, but served as a financial advisory resource for Steve. My role was more like that of a CFO to the organization, helping Steve get NCCH off the ground.

When NCCH opened its doors in early 1985, Steve became its founding president. It was a start-up, and the challenge was finding capital and launching the organization so it could provide services. Steve was a social worker; he knew how to deliver services for disadvantaged people. It made sense for him to handle all the actual group home development. Based upon my background, I became involved with the financing strategy and execution. I complemented him with a strong financial acumen.

Together, we grew the upstart organization, navigated it through rapid growth, and positioned it for sustained growth. This involved lease financing via the state of Ohio, as well as the issuance of bonds and working with senior lenders. The financial piece was very challenging, but I was passionate about the work. Just as important, Steve is one of the finest human beings I have ever been privileged to meet.

Over the years, Steve pioneered the development of safe, comfortable, and affordable homes of high quality for people with developmental disabilities, severe mental illness, or other disabilities. In the process, he became one of Northeast Ohio's best-known advocates for people with disabilities. Steve brought with him to NCCH a combination of passion, integrity, determination, commitment to excellence, persistence in the face of multiple challenges, and an open mind.

It is safe to say that the greatest and most satisfying result of Steve's leadership can be seen in the smiling faces of those who can now live fuller and more independent lives in homes of their own.

NCCH did not staff the homes they operated; rather, the staffing was provided by other nonprofit agencies. NCCH did start another nonprofit that provided staffing services at one point during the journey, but this effort was eventually merged into another agency and allowed NCCH to focus on what it did best.

After serving in the accounting role for several years, Steve asked me to join the board of directors. I was flattered and humbled, but it created a new problem: to join the Board, SS&G had to resign as the outside accountants because of independence and conflict of interest rules. But, I was passionate about the cause—it was more important to me than the actual business of representing NCCH—and accepted the invitation.

I was scheduled to join the board in the mid-1990s. Prior to my first board meeting, I received a call from Steve. The current board chair was having some serious medical issues and could no longer perform the chair duties. Before my first meeting as a board member, Steve asked if I would assume her responsibilities. And that was the beginning of a 10-year assignment as chairman of the board of North Coast Community Homes.

Working with NCCH was an incredibly rewarding and challenging responsibility. The state of Ohio needed us to be successful, so the state was incredibly helpful in the early years. We negotiated sweetheart deals that provided cash flow to support development debt, with lease payments continuing for 18 years after the original debt was paid off in seven years. This strategy carried NCCH in the beginning. We received rental payments from our subsequent tenants, and those allowed us to continue to finance growth and expansion.

As we continued to grow the organization, we started building an internal infrastructure to support operations and provide maintenance to our homes. Our success offered other opportunities in surrounding counties, and we broadened our reach to those with mental illness and the homeless.

In growing, there became a time we could no longer count of the state of Ohio to support us, so we developed our own internal group to seek out philanthropy to support our mission. We hired Barbara Rosenthal to handle the fundraising. And we worked with Barbara to build an infrastructure to support those initiatives—creating a list of people, developing a database, identifying larger potential funders, and working hard to get the NCCH name out in the community.

Our biggest challenges were building enough homes for those in need (which today is still a big number) and fighting off communities that would not welcome us. We were often faced with cities changing the definition of families in their respective charters to prohibit NCCH from developing a home. Without just coming out and saying it, they basically said, "We don't want your people in our community."

On several occasions, I found myself in federal court fighting for our residents. In the end, the various city efforts were always deemed unconstitutional, and were allowed to proceed.

In 1984, we had no homes and no residents, and Steve was our sole employee. Today, we house more than 1,000 mentally challenged individuals in more than 230 homes across six counties. We have a waiting list. And, we have a staff of close to 30 people.

Steve retired a few years ago, and I remain a life trustee. I am very proud of the work we've done together at NCCH. It is one of those organizations built as a labor of love.

WINDING RIVER

CONSULTING

Chapter 8

I NEVER WOULD HAVE BELIEVED—ANOTHER CHAPTER

ACKNOWLEDGEMENTS

I want to thank my new team. Jeannette Schwartz-Ruttan for believing in me and Erica Yesko, Ilana Isakov-Katz, Matt Terlop, and Evan Ishida

* * * * *

The period after SS&G was acquired by BDO was an interesting time in my life. I enjoyed many things about working at BDO, but ultimately being part of such a large firm wasn't a good fit for me. I decided to leave.

I thought my working life would be over once I left, but I was wrong. As my days at BDO were ending, I thought a lot about my father and father-in-law (both successful and accomplished CPAs) who died from Alzheimer's disease. Watching these vibrant men become so debilitated was sobering, and I decided to do everything in my power to avoid that fate. At present, there is no cure for this cruel disease, but there is evidence that staying mentally engaged and physically active are among the best things a person can do to help themselves combat it. I wasn't ready to hang it up.

I left BDO December 31, 2016, and started Winding River Consulting on January 1, 2017. I asked my valued and loyal colleague, Jeannette Schwartz-Ruttan to join me (BDO permitted me to ask her). Jeannette signed on for my next chapter.

Choosing the name Winding River Consulting (WRC) was a process. At first, almost every name I came up with was taken. Of course, Shamis Consulting was available, but I decided I wanted a name not connected to me, so I could possibly build some institutional value.

In many of my presentations I talk about the Private Equity world and how Private Equity consists of a bunch of rich people employing a bunch of Ivy league graduates to buy businesses for them. They name the Private Equity firm after the street they work or live on. I live on a beautiful street on the east side of Cleveland called Winding River Trail. Business is often described as being like a winding river—unexpected turns and changes in current. My newest venture had a name.

I've gotten many positive comments about the name and logo. (Credit for the logo goes to Ilana Isakov Katz, my former marketing director at SS&G, who has been instrumental in launching WRC.)

Off to a great start!

I decided to focus WRC on two industries: accounting and restaurants. Businesses pay a premium on deep industry knowledge, and I certainly know the ins and outs of the two I choose. They were natural choices. In the restaurant industry, I was primarily interested in sitting on corporate restaurant boards and helping with financial strategy projects. On the restaurant side, I landed two restaurant boards and interviewed for several others. I am also working on a sell-side advisory project for a marquee restaurant group on the East Coast. So far, so good.

The consulting side is coming along, and I've added for-profit boards, a CPA firm and a bedding company to my list of responsibilities. I also have several strategy engagements.

On the accounting side, one of the initiatives I started was a boot camp consisting of high-level courses designed to train leaders. These courses aren't leadership training courses. Instead, they are designed to help proven leaders improve and develop their skills. Over the course of three classes, we've graduated 21 managing directors from $10 million to $150 million firms located across the US and Europe. The graduates rate the boot camp 9.4 out of 10. Our fourth, fifth, and sixth boot camps are scheduled to commence in the spring of 2019.

Although our boot camps have been successful, they're taking longer to build than I thought. I envisioned a Field of Dreams. Instead, it's taking a lot of work, effort, and creativity. We're in the start-up phase, which is both challenging and invigorating.

There isn't much I haven't dealt with in the accounting industry. My involvement with The Leading Edge and The Advisory Board gave me many opportunities to help firms with their issues and problems on an ad hoc basis. I wanted to help medium-size-to-large CPA firms develop strategies for dealing with issues such as mergers and acquisitions, growth, human capital, and succession planning. As I thought about this part of my consultancy, I realized that what I'm most passionate about is teaching people to become better managing partners. This has never been done before. There are no formal training programs anywhere to teach people to be managing partners.

In my 27 years as managing partner of SS&G, I managed through ups and downs, successes and failures. I relied on help from our advisory board, advice from random articles and books, commiserating with colleagues in the industry, and logic and intuition to get me through.

Being a managing partner isn't like any other role at an accounting firm. Becoming one is a monumental event. There isn't a lot of time for a learning curve, and, to use a phrase I've used more than once in this book, you don't know what you don't know.

Many issues managing partners face are handled well by the industry's robust practice management community, where participants learn from their peers and topic experts on best practices and contemporary issues. It is the nuances of the firm—its culture, specific idiosyncrasies, how knowledge is transferred from person to person—that make the transition difficult, sometimes even traumatic.

Winding River's Managing Partner Bootcamp (MPB) addresses these issues as well as how to deal with becoming the firm's chief guide and decision maker.

The curriculum, which is based upon my experience, is geared toward making managing partners better at their job. Each course teaches a skill that often falls into the "knowledge gap"—the black hole where your fantasy of a managing partner's job meets the reality of what it really entails. The curriculum is heavily weighted toward learning higher level skills that aren't addressed in traditional practice management venues, such as dealing with difficult conversations, crisis management, presentation skills, team-building and communications.

There are 15 core courses taught over two three-day periods. Class size is limited to between 10 and 12 people, so we can maximize the experience and allow each participant to focus on the issues most important to them.

MPB also includes daily workouts and a session on overall health and wellness. As a managing partner, you are responsible for the many stakeholders and employees at your firm, as well as clients and the community. Maintaining your health and keeping your stress level down is key to your success.

Building on the success we had with the first boot camp, I plan to expand the MPB program to Europe. My good friend Sandy Manson, co-author of my second book *Stratagem*, will be working with me on this. And, I have already been approached by other professional services providers in other industries who are interested.

When I started Winding River Consulting, I predicted that restaurants would take up about one-third of my time, with the rest focused on accounting. Time will tell whether I'm right, or if the current takes me someplace else. I've never been afraid to explore new opportunities, and I'm still curious about how I can make things work better. It's been an interesting journey so far. I'm excited to see how this new venture unfolds.

Part II

LESSONS LEARNED

Chapter 9

PASSION, PATIENCE AND COMMITMENT

When you are an entrepreneur, when you are building a business, you are the point person—the visionary, problem solver, financial guru, good guy, and bad guy. There are a lot of moving parts, and you need to manage them all simultaneously.

It can be stressful, especially at the beginning, when you are making critical decisions that impact and define your survival. Mentors and advisors. Financing. Strategic plan. Hiring and firing.

Your passion is what keeps you going, even in the most difficult circumstances. It takes a certain amount of introspection to recognize the very passion that fuels you, needs to be tempered with patience and commitment. So, here's some of what I've learned along the way:

HARD DECISIONS FALL ON YOUR SHOULDERS

There were many times I felt like I hit the wall. Decisions were too hard to make and the prospect of implementing them seemed even more difficult. One of those times was when I decided to fire most of the staff at Page, Saltz & Shamis. Many of these people had been at the firm for years. I'd know some of them since I was a teenager. They were nice people who were fine for the work they did at the firm as it existed, but they were not the professionals I envisioned working at my firm.

I tried to be fair with severance and the like, but I'm sure that meant little to people who suddenly found themselves job hunting when they thought they'd spend their entire careers at the firm. Still, although I felt terrible on a personal level, I wanted to build a different kind of firm. Maybe I wanted people more like those I'd met at Touche Ross. I wanted a staff that understood a service culture and the benefits of interacting with clients.

It is always difficult to execute these types of decisions. That never changes. Keeping in mind that the decision is a business decision, not a personal one, helps. Following Rebecca Ryan's advice about taking the high road also is helpful.

DO YOU STAY OR GO?

Part of being an entrepreneur is being a leader, and leaders need to act for the good of the business. They need to be able to put their personal feelings aside and make the best decisions for the business. That may mean anything from firing people to stepping down from a well-loved position, as I did at SS&G when I stepped down as managing partner and became a senior partner.

That was a journey not quite like any other I'd been on. Instead of being the person who decided policy, I became someone who had to follow someone else's policies. Always move forward; always learn new things. Take the good with you and build on it.

I thought about my good friend Sandy Manson, Managing Partner of Scotland's Johnston Carmichael. When we met, Sandy was heir-apparent to the then-managing partner. In 2007, when he became managing partner, the former managing partner had to leave the firm. I didn't understand that at the time.

When I stepped down, I began to understand the logic behind that policy. If you stay, you're trying to get the new person into the role. Your intentions are good, but you still cast a long shadow. The firm can get mixed messages, which can be damaging. There is no one right answer to this dilemma.

IT'S IN THE JOB DESCRIPTION

The decisions you make don't always feel good, but they're part of the job description. As the leader, you need to feel in your gut that you're making the best decisions for each given circumstance, and that you always treat everyone with the respect they deserve.

VISION DOESN'T GET THE BUSINESS STARTED

Sometimes, when starting a business, you tend to only think about your vision. That is only a beginning… it doesn't get the business started. The true first step is writing—on paper—the top three to five things that will move the vision from idea to reality. Depending on the situation, this list might include getting financing and doing due diligence (such as market research, assessment of software options, getting expert guidance and advice on transitioning). The underlying text of each item is how you will lead the way toward accomplishing it. Once you've done that, you are the leader of your own endeavor. Congratulations!

BORN LEADERS? NOT NECESSARILY

There's a lot of discussion around whether people are born leaders or can acquire the skills they need. In my experience, it's a mix. No one is born thinking they will be able to create a positive firm culture that trickles down from your office or fire people they've known for years. It takes a lot of thought to do difficult things in a thoughtful and caring way.

Then there is the problem of being an entrepreneur at heart while you are working for someone else. When I look back at my career, the signs of it were there from the beginning. While I was at Deloitte (then-Touche Ross), I had excellent training that informed me as an accountant, more specifically an auditor. I was a disruptor, though, simply because I worked more efficiently. I didn't set out to change their established processes and procedure; it was just that I saw different ways to do things. It was who I was (and am).

I did the same thing when I went to my father's firm, when I grew the restaurant niche at SS&G, through my nonprofit projects, and with Winding River Consulting. I am an entrepreneur.

There are a few key traits that every entrepreneur I know shares. One is the ability to adapt. When I realized our merger with Joe Smith, CPA, wasn't workable, we got out. When we recognized the number of high net worth individuals in our client database, we formed a wealth management entity to serve those clients. Now, with Winding River, we're adjusting the curricula as we go along so we can best meet the wants and needs of our clients.

The second trait is recognizing you don't know everything. You can't. I had a fair amount of experience working with restaurants by the time Brad Saltz approached me. But I was smart enough to know he knew things I didn't. It was our combined knowledge and experience, me as an outside auditor and Brad as a company CFO, that gave us an edge no other firm could match.

The third asset is the ability to remember what it's like to *not* be a leader. That means being open to listening to suggestions and advice from everyone at the company, whatever their level. You're the one who decides whether to act on an idea, but actively listening to others' opinions keeps you from being walled off in a bubble. We all like to be yessed sometimes, but that's not a particularly productive way to lead.

Finally, don't be afraid to be wrong. When I look back at how Engage! Cleveland grew, I see a very crooked path to where we are now. If one road was blocked, we took another. When that didn't work, we moved on.

Many firms today see the value in an entrepreneurial spirit and actively encourage it. If you are fortunate, you are at a firm or a company that does.

Here's my advice: Nurture your passion. This will make you a more well-rounded, happier person. Get the training you need in both technical and soft skills. It may mean personally paying for an advanced degree, a Dale Carnegie course or Toastmasters, but it will be well worth it in the long run.

If your employer doesn't value your spirit, move on. Look for a new employer who will—or go out on your own.

Keep learning and growing. Be open to new ideas. Monitor trends. Keep in mind that there may be hidden value in suggestions that initially seem outrageous.

TEACH OTHERS

Keep teaching is a corollary to the above. I learned the value of a good foundation when I was at Deloitte, and I carry it with me to this day. One of the benefits of teaching others is that you learn along the way. Everyone has their own set of skills and their own way of thinking. Being open to what you can learn is personally beneficial, as well as good for your business. It allows you to delegate the things you aren't so good at or just don't like to do. I need people around me who can execute the details of my vision. It's not that I can't do it, it's that others can do it better and more efficiently. Acknowledging your weaker traits is both empowering and humbling, particularly as you move up in your career and have the resources to delegate.

And, as you become more successful, you must always remember your roots. Reflect upon your start in business and how you felt when you were faced with consequences you didn't cause. Maybe you were the one who got fired because the firm or company you were at couldn't deal with disruption. Perhaps you just envisioned a different kind of firm, maybe a virtual one.

The process still will be hard. You'll still have sleepless nights. But if you can maintain your humanity and compassion, and remain humble, you'll do the right thing for your company, its employees and—most importantly—yourself.

BAGGAGE COMES WITH THE TERRITORY

Here's the thing: all great success comes with a certain amount of baggage. It comes with the territory. Whether you knowingly make a decision that affects others, like the one I made at Page, Saltz & Shamis, or enforce one that is due to outside circumstances, like when SS&G merged in other firms, you have ultimate accountability.

SS&G's experience with its first association is a good example. I don't know for sure, but I imagine the leaders of that association thought we were cocky and hard to deal with. My view is that we saw the future of large CPA firms as national and regional entities rather than local firms. We understood we weren't the right fit for every client in Cincinnati, we were primarily looking for restaurant clients. In our view, there was no conflict. Did that make us hard to work with or visionaries?

These types of situations may not be obvious at first, especially when you start out as an entrepreneur building a completely new endeavor rather than molding an existing business to fit your vision. It is a natural result of growth. The angst of dealing with tough situations comes along with the rewards of being a leader. To paraphrase Harry Truman, the buck stops with you. So, too, does responsibility for the success or failure of the decisions you make.

PATIENCE

We sometimes read about instant success, but most businesses take time to build. SS&G's restaurant niche, one of the largest in the accounting industry, started small and took decades to build. It requires passion, patience and commitment to build a successful enterprise. Sometimes, patience is the hardest to practice. It isn't an attribute associated with entrepreneurs, but it is a necessary aspect of business.

Often, patience goes along with adapting to changes along the way. Markets change. It's inevitable. Look at all the people who owned businesses that failed because technology advanced or trends changed: People who owned sound studios before music started streaming. The entire Blockbuster franchise. Brick and mortar retail stores that ignored consumers' steady march toward Internet shopping. People who saved up to buy taxi medallions only to be faced with competition from Uber and Lyft. The hotel and publishing industries are other examples. If most of these disrupters were people, most of them wouldn't even be considered middle-aged.

Now, even the accounting industry—which is notoriously slow to adapt to change—is looking at drones for conducting audits. Who would have thought this was a possibility even a few short years ago?

As an entrepreneur, part of your job is being aware of what is going on in your industry, as well as business in general. The inability to recognize that change is always around the corner is a big part of the reason accounting firms are scrambling to find exit strategies. It's a big disruption, but it also creates a lot of opportunity for firms looking to expand.

Patience goes along with change. That sounds like an oxymoron, I know, but being nimble enough to change direction takes patience—or at least a version of it. Things don't stay the same, and, as an entrepreneur you need to have the vison to see what's coming and the patience to change course in a way that encourages your staff to follow your lead and shift what they are doing and how they are doing it. This is the crux of patience, passion and commitment. And, along with these three is persuasion, which is something business leaders need to allow them to accomplish their goals.

All of this may sound exhausting, and sometimes it is. But it is also exhilarating. It is the exhilaration in the face of exhaustion that makes you what you are. Entrepreneurs feel a need to take the next step forward because they always see the finish line—even if is around the bend.

PASSION

I've pretty much told you how important passion is to success. Whether you are a CEO, managing partner, member of the C-suite, staff member or administrator, you need to do the best job you can. Having a culture that teaches teamwork and personal responsibility is the best way to earn that kind of commitment. It becomes harder as your business grows, but everyone needs to be valued for what they offer. And that philosophy needs to come from the top. Passion seeps through an organization quickly when everyone feels the same way about the organization and where it's headed.

COMMITMENT

Commitment to making the best decisions can take many forms. It can mean growing larger, staying small, or even merging with another company. Sometimes, the decisions are personally painful, as when SS&G merged with BDO. Other times, they are neutral or easy, as when Page, Saltz & Shamis decided to end its affiliation with Joe Smith's CPA firm.

One of the hardest things entrepreneurs learn is that even the most difficult decisions aren't truly personal, even when they feel that way. Decisions are made for the ultimate good of the business, even if that means a founder must step away.

We see this happen time and time again throughout industry. Apple is just one example that comes to mind. It lost its edge for a while, and then Steve Jobs came back to the company and changed everything.

Remember, you are the steward of the business; you are not its embodiment.

Chapter 10

CONTINUOUS IMPROVEMENT

Monitoring industry trends and developments, assessing how they will impact the firm, and evaluating how to use them to improve the firm's processes, procedures and priorities is imperative to any company's success. The goal is continuously improving the firm and keeping it on the cutting edge. Part of this is also keeping up with new technology trends, legislative initiatives, and anything else that might impact your firm's future.

YOU DON'T KNOW WHAT YOU DON'T KNOW

Keep in mind that you don't have to do it all alone. In fact, you shouldn't. Even if you are at the very beginning of your business, it's a good idea to work with a trusted consultant in areas where you aren't knowledgeable.

When we worked with Jay Nisberg to find us a firm we could acquire in Cincinnati for SS&G, we brought him in for a few reasons. One, we didn't know firms in the area that well. Two, we didn't have a lot of cash to invest, so our options were somewhat limited. Three, this was our first experience with an acquisition and we weren't sure what to expect.

Although the Joe Smith merger failed, it taught us a lot. And, as short as it was, it gave us the opportunity to gain a toehold in the area. We didn't fault Jay for the outcome and worked with him numerous times over the years.

This is the part of the job that's both challenging and energizing. The "fun" part comes after the evaluation and prioritization is finished, when you must convince (and sometimes cajole) the rest of the leadership team to go along with your decisions.

TRENDS

In the world of business, continuously improving your firm may mean deviating from the traditional view of what a firm is. Think about how your organization feels about implementing some of the trends you see in high-performing firms:

Ancillary businesses: It's no longer just tax and audit. Going forward, sticking with those services won't help firms prosper. Future-forward firms recognize these services are becoming more and more computerized and commoditized, so they are moving in different directions. In addition to offering advisory services, they're organizing separate entities.

This can be done in different ways, either under the firm umbrella or as separate businesses. Some ancillary services firms are considering include financial services, marketing, placement, bookkeeping, family offices, payroll and becoming software resellers. We ventured into these waters at

SS&G and were quite successful. In fact, three of our ventures were not part of the BDO merger and continue to be profitable today: Medic Management Group, LLC, formerly SS&G Healthcare, has 200 employees; SS&G Wealth Management retained its name and has 15 employees; and Paytime Integrated Payroll Services has 40 employees.

Just a short time ago, PwC announced it was opening a law firm in Washington, D.C. to attract global business clients. The firm's services won't be offered as stand-alone services, but only in conjunction with the firm's tax services. Is this just another avenue for consulting services? Perhaps. PwC is the first of the Big 4 to announce a separate legal entity. It will be very interesting to monitor where firms take their advisory and consulting businesses.

Recruiting and retention: This is and has been a hot button issue for years. It's a very strange scenario: there aren't enough people coming into the accounting profession and many of those who are don't want to become partners. So, do you hire people with complementary degrees like business administration or economics, or do you continue to insist that only accountants will do?

Another possible obstacle to attracting the people you want is the perception that AI will take over most of the work CPA firms do. It will take over routine tasks, which will change the nature of the work CPAs do, but won't eliminate it. Forward-thinking firms are preparing for this by building their consulting portfolios, as well as their technological capabilities— including data mining. These firms are attracting talent by promoting their vision of the firm of the future.

Management system: Companies always struggle with different management styles. This is a big dilemma across the accounting industry.

Moving a partner up through the ranks is not the only way to go. Barriers have been broken as firms begin to hire CEOs and COOs from the business world to manage them. Other firms are using co-managing partner arrangements.

These examples certainly aren't definitive of what all firms are doing, and they aren't exclusive to firms of a particular size. But it's happening, more often. Here's what these forward-thinking firms have in common: leaders who aren't afraid to try solutions that are different than what's been done in the past.

These leaders aren't deterred when an initiative fails. They simply pick up the pieces, keep what's good and improve the rest. By striving to continuously improve their firms through stretching the limits of their imaginations, they innovate new business paths. They follow their entrepreneurial instincts. And they become trailblazers.

Internally, I always thought we could be better. Periodically, we took different aspects of our business, tore them down to the studs and rebuilt them as a better mousetrap. Over time, we did this in almost every area of the firm.

SS&G was a tax-centric firm that underwent serious expansion. We had offices throughout Ohio and in Chicago. We realized we could operate more efficiently if our processes were standardized across the firm. Doing that would give us the flexibility of sharing work and people throughout the firm.

We asked Michelle Mahle, then a tax service partner, to lead the effort. She agreed to transition most of her clients and focus on standardizing our tax compliance practices and procedures across all offices. It took close to three years to complete the job, and the result was incredible operational efficiencies that increased profitability by a few percentage points.

By doing so, we'd proven the power of improvement internally, and we understood that being recognized by others for our achievements would help our brand. We won many awards as our firm grew and became better known. Among other awards, we received E&Y's Entrepreneur Of The Year Award in 2008. We were also on Crain's list of largest regional firms. Recognition only enhanced our reputation.

Chapter 11

STRATEGIC PLANNING

Planning is critical to success, although that may not be as straightforward as it sounds. I'm not a fan of formal planning. For me, a one-page document that's referred to and reviewed frequently is enough.

Here's an example.

There's a lot in the news about adapting the workplace to accommodate Millennials and members of Generation Z. In my plan, that would fall under something like "employee retention." No specifics. Then, if the most important item that Millennials value is dress code, we can work on that. If it's work/life balance, we'll focus there. It doesn't make much sense to change the firm's dress code if it's not an issue for the staff.

Every one of my entrepreneurial endeavors was built on the same eight building blocks mentioned earlier—and they're all intertwined. That's how I build my strategic plan. If there's too much detail, it's easy to get bogged down and not pay attention to what's really happening at your firm.

A short plan that's easy to adapt works well. Here's an example of how this type of plan can work:

1. Improvements
   a. Technology
      i. What upgrades are most important to implement this year and how much should be budgeted for them?
         1. Hardware
         2. Software
         3. CRM
   b. Business development and marketing
      i. Are we staffed well?
      ii. If we need to hire, who do we need and what's the plan?
   c. Leadership
      i. How is our future leadership pipeline?
   d. Security
      i. Are there cybersecurity issues?

2. Recruiting and retention
   a. What's our retention rate?
      i. Is it higher/lower than last year?
   b. Which recruiting efforts are working best?
   c. Should we consider changing from annual performance reviews?
   d. Are there any problem team members?
   e. Are there any communication issues?
   f. Is there anyone we should give special recognition to for their contributions?

3. Competitive advantage
   a. Have the parameters changed for our target clients?
   b. Have any major clients left?

    i. Why?

    ii. Where did they go?

c. Has any team member, advisory board member, or COI (center of influence) identified any new areas we can expand into?

d. Is there anything our competition is doing in terms of benefits or perks?

    i. Should we implement something new to help us attract and retain talent?

Once the plan is written, develop it further by meeting with key firm leaders and other team members and assigning specific tasks to each of them. Then, monitor how the plan is moving along.

Remember, unless you have unlimited funds and a deep bench, prioritizing is key. Every item on your list is important, but some are more critical than others.

We teach this in our boot camps. It's inevitable that as people get into positions of leadership their day-to-day responsibilities eat their time and they never spend enough time on the planning side. When that happens, it becomes difficult for your vision to move forward.

One of the things we discuss is how to get outside of your bubble. It's about educating yourself in a broad way and bringing those different views back into your firm. Reading non-industry publications is one way. Here's an example: I read an article in the *Wall Street Journal* about self-insuring for health insurance. It sounded like a good idea, so I researched it. As a result, we implemented a firm-wide plan that included a reduced deductible for employees who take an annual physical. We saved millions in premiums over 10 years.

Similar things happen when we have innovative outside people speak at Winning Is Everything and at our Restaurant Boot Camp. We often hear anecdotal evidence about how helpful it is to hear about what is going on outside of our own four walls.

Chapter 12

EXECUTION

It's a fact: nothing happens unless something is accomplished. That sounds overly simple, I know. The truth is, in the real world you are just one person who can only keep track of as many things as your day will allow. There are always crises that take your attention from your to-do list.

Nevertheless, as the firm's ultimate authority, you're in charge of making sure the projects the firm commits to get done in a timely manner. That includes client work as well as undertakings from your strategic planning to-do list. It's not always pretty, but one of your main tasks is making sure the things you want to get done are accomplished. This is why I've always found writing a lengthy strategic plan to be a waste of time. A one- or two-page plan is sufficient. But—and it's a big but—you need to be able to execute the plan. If you can't do that, you'll stay stagnant. That is the crux of the matter: having a plan doesn't mean anything unless you execute it.

Part of good execution is not taking on too much at once. Success doesn't happen overnight. Mostly, it comes in achieving small bites, which I call "strategic initiatives," that move your plan along in a manageable way.

Limiting the number of active strategic initiatives at any given time to no more than four or six allows you to monitor and control progress more efficiently.

The starting point needs to be putting the plan and each of its strategic initiatives in writing, along with the people who are responsible for each step and a timeline. Be nimble—if something isn't working, try something else. Be patient. Sometimes even small bites happen in even smaller ones. Over time, though, you will fulfill your strategic goal.

I didn't learn these lessons overnight. It took time and a certain amount of failure to make me humble enough to recognize them.

We saw this happen in many ways. Making over our tax department took about three years. After doing her analysis of what needed to be done, Michelle Mahle had to get buy-in from the partners, and implement and teach everyone the software. It was a massive undertaking that had three essential components: marketing, capacity and strategy. These same components were part of all our major initiatives. When we deviated, as we did with the Joe Smith merger, things often went badly. When we were strategic, for example with the restaurant vertical, and as we built our ancillary businesses, we were highly successful.

I followed the same process as I built The LEA. We started with a core group, marketed our ideas to them, started with what we considered a manageable number of firms, and stuck with our strategy of giving them access to other like-minded firms. Once we saw it working, we used the same plan to build out an international presence.

Failure is an inevitable part of success. The important thing is not letting your ego lead the project. Even though you're the managing partner or CEO, you must be open to exploring different ways of doing things. Sometimes things move along quickly. That's a bonus. Mostly, success involves doing things more slowly and methodically than your entrepreneurial spirit finds comfortable.

GARY SHAMIS

Chapter 13

ACCOUNTABILITY

Accountability—taking responsibility for the good and bad in a business—might be the biggest factor in an entrepreneur's success. We all want to be right all the time, but no one is. Most of us make many mistakes in our lives.

The difference between success and failure is what you do when you make a poor choice. If you're someone who picks up his/her marbles and goes home if things don't go your way, you don't have the right temperament to be an entrepreneur. But if you have the motivation to accept responsibility for a misstep, assess what went wrong and keep trying, you might be great.

When you're the one in charge of a business, you are the point person—the one people look to as the final decision maker. It's an awesome responsibility. If you are a one-person business, you're responsible for making enough money to sustain yourself and your business. As the business grows and you hire other people, you need to be able to take care of them, too.

It can be challenging, especially when you get to the point where you're taking on someone at a professional or C-suite level. Remember when my father enticed me to come to his firm by offering me the same salary I'd been earning in Atlanta? That was a huge commitment for him—but I didn't know that until I came on board and realized if I wanted to keep earning that salary I'd have to bring in new accounts to support it.

Building a space to expand into? You need to be able to get the financing and pay the mortgage.

The same is true when you invest in technology.

Sometimes it's a horse-before-the-cart scenario. But you, as the "father or mother of the business," are accountable for these decisions. You'd better be darn sure you'll be able to meet your commitments, and you can only do that by having a carefully thought out strategic plan and good forecasting.

In the short term, it may mean you need to take a salary cut, forgo a bonus, or put off getting new office furniture. When we decided to build a building for SS&G in Solon, Ohio, I had to take a big cut in salary for a while. The choice was doing that and having a 10,000-square foot headquarters building we could call our own, or continue renting bigger and bigger spaces as we grew. For us, the path was clear.

You're accountable for the bottom line, so the decisions you make, at least at the beginning of the business's life, fall into two categories: need and want. You need to hire high-level people because they are the life blood of your success. My father's firm would have stayed a small mom-and-pop firm without my vision. If I didn't hire Brad Saltz to lead SS&G's restaurant niche, we may not have become an industry leader in that area. The situation was similar when I hired Karen Kehl-Rose at LEA, Jen Chestnut at Hillel, and Ilana Isakov Katz and Jeannette Schwartz at Winding River. These entities continue moving forward because talented people are in place doing the things they do better than I.

Spending money on good people, the right people for the job, is the highest priority for any thriving business. That includes salary and benefits, of course, as well as opportunities for learning and access to the best technology. If that means you, as the leader, need to take a real or metaphorical pay cut, the result will be worth your sacrifice.

Something relatively new that entrepreneurs deal with daily is the changing workforce. Years ago, someone could open a retail clothing store and call themselves an entrepreneur. And they were. They led the business and ensured its viability. The people who worked for them were loyal—as long as they were treated right.

That's not true today. We see that in the way firms are adapting to what younger workers want and expect from their workplace. Everything from flextime to remote work to a relaxed dress code to changes in how feedback is given are being reviewed in firms and companies across the country.

In a sense, it is this way because the entrepreneurial spirit is alive in all of us to varying degrees. The best employees want to learn and grow. Finding ways to nurture this need while creating loyalty to your company is challenging. Nevertheless, I can't say this enough: Your people are your greatest asset, and investing in them is the best thing you can do to assure the success and continuity of your business.

One of the best ways to do this is by holding them accountable for meeting the requirements outlined in their job descriptions—and for meeting any additional responsibilities or learning initiatives they sign up to take on. That doesn't mean you, or they, won't take a wrong step. But it does mean you're responsible for overseeing what they are doing. You are accountable to each other.

When I realized our merger with Joe Smith, CPA was not working, I met with Brad Saltz, got his input, and decided to end the arrangement at the tail end of the contractual time we had to reverse the merger. We took the good stuff we learned with us, including a budding restaurant niche and a lot of knowledge about what a good merger should look like.

The situation was similar when I envisioned LEA. It wasn't enough to want an association with a particular set of attributes. We were successful because we mapped a strategy built on our perception of what other associations did wrong and executed on it.

Success, therefore, is a team effort that needs to be baked into every aspect of your company's culture. As you grow, you won't be able to oversee everything and everyone. Still, you're the face of the firm. As such, you're accountable for its overall performance as well as the actions of your employees.

The company culture begins with you; you are the model. Taking responsibility for your actions, as well as those of your partners and staff, isn't always easy, but it is your duty as the company's leader.

Chapter 14

PEOPLE, PEOPLE, PEOPLE

Once you are no longer operating as a solo, having the right people in place matters more than almost anything else. What position will you hire for first? Why? And, how will you find the right person?

I've always believed in hiring people who have the right skills. They may or may not have held the same position, but the people you hire need to have a reputation for understanding the position.

Karen Kehl-Rose is a great example of why this tactic works. Karen was hired as Executive Director of The Leading Edge Alliance, even though she never held a similar position. She had been the Vice President of Member Services at the Illinois Society of CPAs, though, and that meant she understood the profession and the psyche. We looked at the skills and attributes she brought with her, not the name of the position she held. It was a great decision. And she has managed to navigate a complicated position since she was hired.

Brad Saltz is another example of a good hire. A CPA who worked in industry, rather than at a firm, Brad didn't have the direct experience many firms would have required. I looked at it differently: He was a good accountant, and I wanted to develop a niche in the restaurant industry. His knowledge of daily restaurant operations and the how-tos of developing a growth strategy for a restaurant franchise was valuable to our firm's goals. Hiring him was crucial to SS&G's success in the restaurant industry.

Rebecca Ryan is another person who helped put the firm on the track to success. Her advice about how to provide a workplace attractive to millennials was invaluable. So were her leadership tips. They taught me how to manage my time more effectively and deal with tough situations more compassionately.

It isn't enough to look at your business as an entrepreneur's idea come to life. You need to let your instincts guide you in making good hiring decisions. I'm not saying hiring a restaurant person from another firm or an executive director from another association would have meant failure. It probably wouldn't have, but the pace may have been slower or more difficult. I am also not saying you don't need good staff or administration people to support them. Everyone does. What I am saying is each of these endeavors benefitted from the guidance they got from people with a different point of view. Karen and Brad brought their unique experiences with them and massaged what they knew to fit the position that they were entrusted with.

Those are the success stories. Unfortunately, there have been other times it hasn't worked out so well—but it's all part of growing and running a business. Sometimes you just must be ballsy, like I was when I first took over my father's firm and fired nearly the entire staff. Over the years, I've had to make other similar decisions. Each of them required a certain amount of introspection, so I could be sure personal feelings were not part of the equation. And, each of these, in their own way, left its scar.

When a hire is not a good fit, either for cultural, skill set or some other reason, the best thing you can do is end the relationship as quickly as possible.

It is never easy to do this, especially with a high-level hire or someone you know personally. But making the best decisions for the business is your priority. From the moment you recognize the fit is wrong, start documenting relevant dates, times and actions. Then consult with an attorney to make sure you aren't violating any employment laws. It's important to have this information ready in case the person decides to sue.

This is one part of the preparation. The other side is giving feedback to the person so that the termination discussion doesn't come as a complete shock. Actual termination discussions are hard. There is no other way to say it, and there is no way to avoid the unsettled feelings you'll have. But there are some things you can do to make the meeting a little easier, and for lack of another term, a bit safer from litigation.

- Have a second person with you in the room to serve as a witness to the conversation.

- Plan to keep the conversation short and general. Say something like "the company is going in a different direction" rather than "you aren't a good fit."

- Have any documents that need to be signed (e.g., confidentiality agreement, separation settlement) available at the meeting.

- Be prepared to ask the person to leave immediately and hand over any electronic devices, keys, or other pieces of company property that is in their possession.

Whichever side of this discussion you are on, you will be left with impressions that carry forward to other business decisions. For example, when the first association we were with terminated our membership, I began thinking about the kind of association I wanted to be with. I didn't act on it for a while because there were other priorities. But in that moment, the germ of The Leading Edge was born.

Similarly, we never again entered into a merger agreement using the same logic we used when we merged in Joe Smith's firm. How we handled our desire to have a presence for SS&G in New York City is a good example. We learned and grew, and we tried never to make the same mistake twice.

Chapter 15

COMPETITIVE ADVANTAGE

Competitiveness is a big part of the picture. Think about how you got where you are now. Being competitive probably is part of who you are. When you are a business leader, though, you need to channel this trait. You must be as competitive with yourself as you are with the businesses that are your actual competitors—but you need to do it in a way that moves the business forward and creates a positive company culture. Think about it. I call it "conscious competitiveness," and for me it has five main components:

1. SET INCREMENTAL GOALS

You're training for a triathlon, not running a sprint. Setting small goals as you move forward allows you to take a step back and assess the landscape for any changes that will affect your business.

These changes may be anything, from the loss of your biggest client to a key partner dying or retiring unexpectedly to your next-in-command deciding to take a new position. For me, the decision to open a Cincinnati office so I could hire Brad Saltz was an excellent decision. When our association with the first CPA firm alliance didn't work out, I tried a second one. It wasn't my best decision, but it made me aware that the best course of action for our firm was to found our own alliance. Even then, though, we started small, with only a handful of U.S. firms.

Any of these changes, or any of the million and one other things that can occur, gives you the opportunity to reassess. Is the change due to a natural life stage, something that you can change to make your company more appealing—such as a higher salary or greater delegation of responsibility—or is it dissatisfaction with client service?

Once you do your analysis, you can reset your goals to accommodate the change and keep moving ahead. It is harder to be nimble and adjust if your goals are too high.

I've dealt with this in different ways at different times. Perhaps my most successful strategy was setting 40,000-foot "umbrella goals," and having more achievable goals as each smaller goal was achieved.

2. WHEN YOU ARE MAKING CHANGES, WIN OVER SUPPORTERS ONE AT A TIME

Suppose you decide to bring in a practice leader from outside of your firm. Plan how you're going to gain the backing of the people in the division. What about the manager who was passed over for promotion? What kind of hole will it leave if that person leaves your firm?

Your decision may be the best one for the firm. It may even boost the firm's competitiveness in the marketplace. But inevitably, there will be people who view it as disrespectful to the person they thought would move up into the position. You need to have a Plan B, and maybe even a Plan C, in place to deal with any repercussions.

You're the leader. Not everyone is going to like you, and you shouldn't care. Your business is your baby; it's your job to prioritize its needs.

3. CELEBRATE SUCCESS

Success takes many forms. Celebrate all of them—appropriately. We celebrated when we got out of our toxic merger. We celebrated The Leading Edge's success; the completion of the Hillel at Kent State; and every other benchmark that was important to us. Smaller successes need to be recognized, too: promotions; the implementation of a new CRM; an employee's five-year anniversary with the firm; the end of tax season; and special achievements like passing the CPA exam.

Events like these are good things. They give everyone the opportunity to get together and be happy about someone or something. If you've done a great job creating a positive culture, use these celebrations as a time to mingle with people at all levels. Take note of how they look and act when you speak with them. They shouldn't look frightened when you engage them in conversation.

Spend your time listening to unspoken signals: Do people seem happy to be there? How long do they stay? Are different levels of the firm interacting or are there cliques?

These are some clues to whether the real, on-the-ground culture at your firm is working or not.

4. USE FAILURE AS A SPRINGBOARD, NOT AN END

What is failure? Was my father's CPA firm a failure because it only had small business clients and no real aspirations to grow? Thousands of firms around today still follow that model. Were Hillel and Engage! Cleveland failures because they took so long to build? Was SS&G's road to an association that met its needs a failure?

None of these entities failed. They all succeeded, in their own time, for different reasons, and sometimes as a different entity then originally envisioned. Here's what they have in common: passionate belief in the cause that sustained them through all the dead ends.

We kept trying different things. We knocked on doors and met with experts to get help, input and new ideas. We didn't stop trying until we found a path forward that worked. Each path was unique. The commonality was that I, as the leader, was engaged in seeing the entity come to life.

5. RESPECT EVERYONE EQUALLY

No one is worth more than anyone else. Some people are richer or smarter or have easier access to opportunities than others, but that doesn't mean they are better. Think about some people who've come up from poor or middle-class backgrounds and succeeded: Jay Z; Dolly Parton; Mark Cuban; Kat Cole; Derek Jeter. People listen to them now, but that wasn't always the case. Each of them had passion for what they were doing and kept trying—even when they failed. Sometimes, people with the right attributes fail right into success.

Remember, there is no such thing as instant success. Pieces of the endeavor may be instantly successful, like when I met with the original firms of The Leading Edge Alliance to talk about the need for a new association. But that's not the whole story. It never is. Sometimes, parts come together easily; it's figuring how to glue them together permanently that takes planning and perseverance.

Chapter 16

TRANSPARENCY

Your business is your baby. You love it, nurture it and sacrifice for it. To make it work, though, you also need to be open to new ideas—ideas that don't necessarily come from you.

To be successful, this means you need to park your ego at the door and be receptive to the ideas, opinions and criticisms of other people—mentors, co-workers and clients. Let's face it, no one gets to a leadership position without a certain amount of ego. It's normal and healthy. The trick is not letting your ego override good decision-making.

All of this relates back to the company culture. Do you want to be a leader who leads through dictate and fear, or one who is looked up to as someone who is fair and approachable? Put that way, it sounds contrived: the "right" answer is the latter. For some of us, though, it takes a lot of conscious effort not to hold our baby so close that we suffocate it. Don't get me wrong, many successful firms have fairly autocratic leaders. It's a model which has worked well for many years. Until the Baby Boomers like me came into the workplace, people were conditioned to listen to their bosses and wait their turn to become one. But the shift in generational views between Boomers and the generations that came before them was obvious, simply because of the size of the cohort. The same thing is happening with the Millennials; they became the largest cohort in the workplace in 2015, and are now poised to take over leadership roles on a large scale. Generation Z, and its generational characteristics, are starting to enter the workforce. Adaptations will have to be made for them as well.

Combined with these generational shifts are rapid changes in technology, including robots, drones, trends toward remote and part-time work (despite pushback from some major corporations), cybersecurity and global economic and political changes. These are just the tip of the iceberg, so to speak. Each one has far-reaching implications for different areas of a business. Spend some time reading about what some experts think. I recommend *The Seventh Sense* by Joshua Cooper Ramo (Hatchette 2016) and *The Originals* by Adam Grant (Viking 2016).

The mix of highly disruptive changes are deeply affecting peoples' expectations about life and work. As business leaders and entrepreneurs, we must look at these changes with curiosity and openness.

Making a shift to a more inclusive, transparent model is necessary to accommodate the new business environment. It's complicated, for sure. And none of it takes away from the fact that you have ultimate accountability for what happens to and in your company. You are the Harry Truman of your world: the buck stops with you.

EPILOGUE

The ups and downs, highs and lows of every entrepreneur's journey are different. There is no one right or wrong. No perfect path. No black and white.

What is clear is that achieving your goals is exhilarating. It's a feeling relatively few individuals achieve. I'm lucky to be one of them, and I wish you a path without too many hurdles and a lifetime of learning and growing.

Now, go out and take charge of your life. Build something. Anything. By doing so, you will find that you, too, can achieve your goals.

ACKNOWLEDGEMENTS

The first eight chapters of this book would not have happened without the help of many wonderful people.

The first eight chapters also didn't happen without the support and understanding of my family—my wife Mary Ann; my children Ben, Nicole, Melissa and Eli; and my grandson Max and granddaughter Ruby. Thank you for being so patient and giving me the time I needed to succeed.

I would also like to thank my three assistants, who always made me look good: Marlene Ritter (of blessed memory), Tricia Schaefer-Anto and Jeannette Schwartz-Ruttan (who continues on the journey).

This book was not possible without the help and encouragement of Marsha Leest, and the last push by Dustin Klein.

This book is intended to inspire and guide any entrepreneur looking for the same experienced guidance.

ABOUT THE AUTHOR

Gary Shamis is the CEO of Winding River Consulting. An award-winning serial entrepreneur, he is also the founder and chairman emeritus of LEA Global, the second-largest international professional association; co-founder and partner of The Advisory Board, a CPA firm think tank; and co-founder and host of Winning is Everything  Conference, the Advisory Board's annual proprietary management conference.

Prior to founding Winding River, Shamis spent 35 years building SS&G into one of the nation's largest, fastest-growing, and most respected accounting and consulting firms in the country. It was ranked as the thirty seventh largest firm by *Accounting Today* before it was combined with BDO USA LLP in 2015.

His innovative leadership has earned Shamis recognition as an Ernst & Young "Entrepreneur of the Year" and "Top Ten Managing Partner Elite" by *Accounting Today*, among other industry accolades. He's served his profession within the ranks of Ohio Society of CPAs (OSCPA) and the American Institute of Certified Public Accountants (AICPA), and is active in more than two dozen nonprofits.

Additionally, Shamis writes and edits for industry journals and has co-authored two books, *How to Manage Your Accounting Practice: Taking Your Firm from Chaos to Consensus* (2009) and *Stratagem: Simple, Effective Strategic Planning for Your Business and Your Life* (2013).

He holds a Master of Accountancy degree from The Ohio State University and a Bachelor of Science degree in Biology from Tulane University.